4

WITHDRAWN

GOD AND THE SELF

GOD
AND THE SELF

Three Types
of Philosophy of Religion

Wayne Proudfoot

Lewisburg
Bucknell University Press
London: Associated University Presses

Associated University Presses, Inc.
Cranbury, New Jersey 08512

Associated University Presses
108 New Bond Street
London W1Y OQX, England

Library of Congress Cataloging in Publication Data

Proudfoot, Wayne, 1939–
  God and the self.

  Bibliography: p.
  Includes index.
  1. Religion—Philosophy.   I. Title.
BL51.P74   200'.1   75-28983
ISBN 0-8387-1769-1

Reprinted by Permission of New York University Press: extracts
from *Religious Experience and Truth: A Symposium,* edited by
Sidney Hook, © 1961 by New York University.

Contents

Preface

This book originated in a curiosity about the various options prevalent in modern philosophies of religion and the criteria for choosing among those options. My initial interest in such an inquiry arose from reflection on the reasons for the adoption of certain positions with particular metaphysical and theological implications by some persons and not by others. Why do mystical traditions seem so distant from my own experience, while they are immediately appropriated by friends and colleagues? Why does each of the types described in the book seem appropriate at different moments, in connection with different experiences, and at different stages in the life of an individual? My interest was increased by a consideration of the issues and methods involved in teaching aspects of the study of religion to classes of students who represented widely divergent backgrounds. Different models and images called for different modes of presentation, and were attractive and compelling to different constituencies.

These questions led to the attempt to correlate types of *Weltanschauungen* and their metaphysical and theological implications with different aspects of experience and of psychosocial development. While the questions raised above are not directly answered here, the correlation between types of finite-infinite relation and emphases upon particular aspects of experience suggests that a certain metaphysical option will be compelling to those who share a focus on the aspects of experience and of psychosocial development to which that option gives clearest expression.

7

My thoughts about diverse ways of perceiving the world, and the selection for emphasis of different elements of experience, were first stimulated by Carol Proudfoot and Herbert Richardson. I want to express my appreciation to them for the experiences and insights that gave rise to this project. I would like to thank Richard R. Niebuhr, Gordon Kaufman, and William R. Rogers for reading and commenting extensively on an early draft. George Rupp has been a close friend and colleague throughout the period during which these ideas were developed. Many conversations with him during the early stages provided encouragement, critical response, and an impetus toward clarity. Finally, I want to thank my wife, Ruth Ellen Proudfoot, for support without which these ideas might not have been formed into a book, and for introducing me to the world of contemporary social psychology.

Acknowledgment is due to the following publishers for permission to quote from copyrighted material:

Adam and Charles Black, from Austin M. Farrer, *Finite and Infinite*, 2d ed., 1959, and *The Glass of Vision*, 1948, both Dacre Press, A & C Black, Ltd.
The University of Chicago Press, from Paul Tillich, *Systematic Theology*, vols. 1–3, 1951–1963, and *The Protestant Era*, ed. James Luther Adams, 1948.
A brief statement of the typology presented in chapter 1, and of the general argument of the book, appeared in the *Journal of Religion* 55(1975):57–75, and is used here by permission of the editors of the *Journal*, published by the University of Chicago Press.

GOD AND THE SELF

1

Introduction

In recent years, students of religion and theology have turned increasingly to the social sciences for illumination concerning the nature of human existence and the development and function of religious symbols and institutions. The study of religion had previously been informed primarily by the work of philosophers, who had articulated and attempted to answer the questions that arise when issues and problems are extrapolated to their broadest horizons. Questions concerning the nature of being, the meaning and end of history, the origin and transformations of human consciousness, and the search for a highest good or first cause were all raised under the auspices of philosophy. Theologians felt a special kinship with this philosophical tradition and borrowed particular tools and formulations from it, though some maintained that they had access to an additional resource that the philosopher either did not possess or had overlooked in his role as philosopher. Revelation provided the insight that closed the circle, completed the *Gestalt,* or capped the system of truth.

Philosophy is no longer a single discipline covering all human queries, though it is still true that philosophical issues are broached whenever any discipline is driven to question its own first principles or to scrutinize its language. During the nineteenth and early twentieth centuries, philosophy was increasingly differentiated from the scientific study of persons and societies. This differentiation was aided by the developing practice of dividing university faculties into departmental units, within which graduate training took place. This differentiation proceeded apace. The result is often a compartmentalization of issues that were fruitfully combined and interwoven in the work of figures such as William James, Wilhelm Dilthey, and Max Weber.

At the present time there is a growing appreciation on the part of both philosophers and social scientists of the fact that this differentiation has its liabilities as well as its assets. Research in the sociology of knowledge has provided an understanding of the structures of social life that give rise to certain ideas and symbolic systems. At the same time, some social scientists and philosophers are beginning to raise essentially philosophical questions about the presuppositions that underlie various theoretical and empirical approaches to the study of human behavior. Philosophers have attended closely to the structure and function of natural languages, a pursuit that involves them in the study of the most pervasive and nuanced of social and cultural institutions. Social scientists are becoming increasingly aware of the cognitive components of attitudes, emotions, and behavior, which some had hoped to describe and to explain without reference to mental activity.

The mutual interaction between research in the social sciences and philosophical reflection has been especially appreciated by students of religion. While theologians have traditionally been preoccupied with their relation to philosophy, it is impossible to deny the fact that religions are composed of symbols, behavior, and institutions that are integral parts of cultural, social, and psychological systems. In the initial rush to appropriate the methods and materials of social science for the study of religion and culture, however, some have been uncritical in this appropriation and have attempted to replace philosophical scrutiny with what is purported to be an objective and value-free social scientific approach. It is clear that the tools of each of several disciplines can contribute to the study of religion. The difficulty lies in discovering the appropriate tools for the consideration of different issues.

This study is an investigation of several philosophical conceptions of God and the self, with particular attention to the interpretation of the significance of these conceptions in the light of our knowledge of human development and activity, and with attention to the particular aspects of experience that are highlighted by each. There is no attempt here to reduce philosophical conceptions or issues to some allegedly more fundamental categories that are appropriate to the social sciences. Research in the social sciences can, however, illumine the issues under consideration in two ways. First, since we are studying conceptions of the self and claiming that different notions of God are correlated with different views of the self, it is possible that psychological and sociological research may be of assistance in evaluating the different conceptions. Second, theories of cognitive development in the growth of individuals and societies may provide insight into the appearance at certain points in the developmental process of particular conceptions of the self and God. It is an assumption of this work that ideas or conceptions are rooted in experience and that they have consequences for future experience. The choice between divergent philosophical and theological conceptions need not be an arbitrary one. Each has its roots and implications, which can be discovered and examined.

In Occidental religious traditions, the idea of monotheism and the idea of the unity of the self have been closely related, though their relation has not often been explicitly considered. In this study a typology is proposed of several ways in which conceptions of God can be correlated with particular views of the self. Implications of the several types are explored, and each type is evaluated with respect to its adequacy as an expression of particular aspects of religious experience, and with respect to its promise for an adequate understanding of the concept of the self and for the illumination it might provide for the concept of God.

The chief concern of the book is with the correlation

between ideas of God and moments in the development of the self, and with the way in which this correlation is expressed by different conceptions of the relation between finite and infinite. The project stems from the conviction that such ideas as those of God, the self, and the relation between finite and infinite are deeply rooted models and images that may be correlated with the decisions, events, and activities of the persons and communities by which they are entertained. Ideas arise from and are invested with the power of specific human interests and situations. This power returns as those ideas, myths, self-conceptions, and goals influence perception and activity. Such conceptions as those of God and the self give meaning to the interests from which they arise both by shaping themselves to those interests and by shaping those interests to themselves. Clifford Geertz has noted that such symbols serve both as "models of" and "models for" reality.[1] They are at once descriptive and prescriptive. They are interpretations of past and present experience that have important implications for future perception and action.

One of the most fundamental and complex levels of human symbolic activity is the use of language. Students of religion have long been concerned with the ways in which religious and theological language is related to the experiences out of which it comes and to which it gives rise. Is language adequate to the heights and depths of human experience, and particularly to those aspects of experience which men have held to be religious? Some have claimed that true religious experience is characterized by an immediate relation to the religious object that eliminates the need for or the possibility of articulating that relation in language or any other medium. The prominence of the notion of the Word in Jewish and Christian religious traditions has meant that this concern with the role of language and its relation to religious experience has been unavoidable. Sometimes, as we shall see, the Word and other religious symbols have been interpreted in nonlinguistic fashion in order to maintain the claim that religious experience is unmediated.

In the past several years there has been a resurgence in some sectors of contemporary culture of the advocacy of immediacy in experience. Claims for authenticity and for new paths to self-knowledge as well as to more intimate encounters with others have been made for sensitivity training, for encounter groups of various kinds, and for experiences induced with the aid of pharmacological agents, music, or various physical regimens. Purporting to transcend the "myth of the objective consciousness," these claims have often stressed the nonverbal aspects of experience. When words are employed in such contexts, they are often words of ejaculation, of command and response, or of address. Or they might serve as words or images that are meant to complement the lights, the drugs, or the music as an addition to the multi-media catalyst to a nonverbal experience. They are not words intended to analyze or to synthesize. Words in these contexts are employed in nonverbal ways. They are employed as symbols, rather than as units in a syntactical linguistic structure.

Such claims for the priority of nonverbal experience are not new, of course, and some would claim that they are essential to an understanding of the experience of the sacred or the holy, which is basic to the religions of man. In the last several decades, though, these claims seem to have met new needs, and to be peculiarly attractive to those in Occidental traditions in which overwhelming emphasis has been placed on the verbal aspects of experience, on discrimination, the fixing of boundaries, the identity of the person, and the development of notions of personal responsibility and history.

In other parts of the culture, under the influence of Madison Avenue and the ubiquity of advertising, words have also been employed in nonverbal ways. There is ample occasion for dismay on the part of the teacher or student who is convinced that words and ideas are important and reflect on the ability of persons to make needed discriminations in their own lives and constructions of the world. News media and advertisements report "revolutions" in everything from cosmetics to education. People have long since become accustomed to the fact that words do not mean what they might appear to mean at face value. "Pacification" means destruction. Examples could be multiplied. The point is not so much that words are used to mean their opposites. It is rather that this situation has become so commonplace that it often goes unnoticed. Most persons who listen to an official news conference, read a statement from a bureaucratic agency, watch a televised advertisement, or listen to a sermon do not expect the language to mean what it would appear to mean if the words were taken at face value. The discrepancy arouses little attention.

Many have not been able to discover communities of meaning in their own experience. The task of developing one's own autonomy and independence and the negotiation of new relationships and more complex forms of community has seemed too great. One response has been to derogate verbal skills and discrimination and to espouse a return to immediacy of expression and to the nonverbal. This response is expressive of the situation in which these persons find themselves, though it does not lead to an accurate understanding of the world in which they live. Not only is it based on a false account of the world and the ways in which language functions in experience, but it is an attempt to recover an earlier period of childhood or cultural history that cannot be recovered.

The argument set forth in the following pages for the superiority of the social conception of the self and society implies that pure, unmediated experience is impossible. It is significant that the popularity of the nonverbal has increased markedly in our culture in the last several years. It is possible that a retreat from the verbal to the nonverbal represents a kind of regression and urge to return to immediate contact with the primal source or ground of one's being or with another individual. The complexities of contemporary culture and politics have been such as to cause many to seek for meaning in some form of immediate relation to the cycles of nature, to the rhythms of the cosmos, to psychedelic experience, or to the ideal encounter between ego and thou. Each is envisioned as a kind of touchstone, a guarantee of something real, of meaning in a social and cultural environment in which the forming of intimate relationships and the achievement of personal unity that has an end or telos appear increasingly difficult.[2]

THE CORRELATION OF IDEAS OF SELF AND GOD

A self develops over against and in correlation with a world. The study of language and of the development of cultures illumines the various ways in which notions of the self in a particular society are affected by the culture that is shared by members of that society. Similarly, conceptions of God reflect individual experiences as well as social values and cultural constructs. While it may appear natural that different conceptions of God characterize diverse cultures, it might not be clear that conceptions of the self, seemingly something of which we have direct and immediate knowledge, diverge as fully. The issue of whether knowledge of the self is any more direct or immediate than knowledge of God, and the consideration of how conceptions of self and God are constructed, will be central to the consideration of each of the types presented in the following pages. The classic statement of the parallel status of conceptions of God and the self as ideas of reason is given in Kant's critical analysis of the limits of reason. The correlation between notions of self and God, however, is deeply rooted in the history of theism.

The suggestion that the ideas of self and God are correlative has a long history in Jewish and Christian thought. In

Genesis man is said to be created in the image of God (Gen. 1:26–27, 5:1–3, 9:5–6). Paul speaks of the image of God into which believers enter through faith in Christ (Rom. 8:28).[3] Augustine's use of autobiographical reflection to inform and to dramatize his quest for God, and the place of memory in his understanding of the Trinity are examples of the way in which knowledge of the self has been understood to qualify knowledge of God, and vice versa. In the *Ethics*, Spinoza describes the path toward knowledge of substance (*Deus sive natura*) as increasing knowledge of the self. As persons come to know themselves and the forces that determine them, they become increasingly aware of the full scope of reality or substance. Parochial knowledge is broadened to the point of contemplation of the total scope of substance, which is God. The mystical tradition of contemplation and inner focus until one passes through the dark night of the soul embodies in practical terms the idea that knowledge of God is approached through knowing oneself and that one is able to know oneself fully only in relation to God. In Indian philosophy, *Brahma* and the *atman* are identified.

One of the most explicit statements of this correlation in the history of Christian thought appears in the first sentence of the first book of John Calvin's *Institutes of the Christian Religion*.

> Nearly all the wisdom we possess, that is to say, true and sound wisdom, consists of two parts: the knowledge of God and of ourselves. But, while joined by many bonds, which one precedes and brings forth the other is not easy to discern.[4]

Calvin proceeds then to set forth a theology constructed upon the careful correlation of the knowledge of God and the knowledge of the self.

It is important to note that Calvin speaks of *knowledge* of God and *knowledge* of man as joined. In contrast, the Priestly author of the first chapter of Genesis wrote of man's having been created in the image of God. Here the correlation is not between knowledge of the self and knowledge of God but between the self and God. Irenaeus interpreted the image as the rationality and freedom that are characteristic of human nature. Augustine, in the *Confessions*, wrote of himself in terms of his memory and knowledge of himself. By shifting the emphasis from a statement about human nature to memory and his own knowledge, Augustine prepared the way for critical reflection on the self and its knowing. This critical reflection was clearly articulated by Descartes, who argued that it is possible for a thinker to doubt all knowledge except that of himself thinking and doubting. Hume followed with the suggestion that much of the order discovered by men observing their world is the product of the men who are observing and thinking and of their culture. Notions of order and causation that are created in the mind of the observer by association are illegitimately attributed to the world that is being observed. In *The Natural History of Religion*, Hume suggested that religion and the gods are human hopes and fears writ large and attributed to the cosmos. The Kantian critique of metaphysics and of the traditional arguments for the existence of God elaborated Hume's suggestion of the activity of the human mind in its knowing, and focused the issue with which we are concerned as the correlation of the *idea* of God with the *idea* of the self. The correlation was not now sought between two external things as it was in Genesis and Irenaeus, nor between an idea and its object, but was sought in the process of the self coming to know itself and its world.

The ideas of the self and God, as well as the idea of the world, were thought by Kant to have a parallel status. They are ideas that reason is driven toward, but they can never attain the status of knowledge. They are limiting ideas that serve to orient reason in its organization of our experience. It may seem natural to some to view the notion of God as a limiting idea by which reason orients itself, while the self is seen as something of which we have direct and immediate experience. But Kant held that the ideas of both God and the self are transcendental, or stand at the limits of our experience. It is not that the idea of God reflects events and conflicts that properly belong to the tangible world of the self and its environment, as is held by those who would interpret religion as a simple projection of material desires and forces. God, self, and world are ideas that are constructed in the activity of the experiencing subject. The self is not a privileged reality in contrast with which knowledge of everything else in human experience is slippery and untrustworthy. That was the Cartesian position in the *Meditations*, though even Descartes conceived the mind as ultimately dependent upon God. Kant skillfully argued the impossibility of an appeal to the self as an immediate datum of experience.[5] The self and God are not distinguishable as tangible given and metaphysical notion. They are both ideas that appear in and that regulate the flux of daily experience.

This study can be read as a consideration of various ways of conceiving unity. It is an examination of the relations between monotheistic faith and the intuition of the unity of a person and of the world of which that person is a part. Monotheism and the question of the unity of the self are two themes that are essentially related but that have not often been distinguished and discussed as such. Traditional Christian doctrines such as the doctrine of creation and that of the kingdom of God are unifying concepts, though they may also serve other functions. These doctrines provide cosmological and teleological conceptions of unity.

Theological conceptions of the self and its relation to God exemplify the ways in which religious thinkers have dealt with the classical and universal problem of the one and the many. How are individuals related to wholes? What is the status of an individual, a relation, or a whole? This is an issue with which persons have dealt since the earliest days of mythology and philosophy. It is also an issue with which each individual must struggle in the development of his own identity. Each new perception, each thought, is integrated in such a way that the perceiver or thinker is able to maintain his or her own identity as a self or agent. This unifying process is accomplished through the activity of the imagination in experience. Some integration or unification is necessary in order for experience to occur. Words mean nothing unless they can be integrated in some fashion that is familiar to the reader or listener. This integration may be effected by consulting a dictionary, by another person who serves as interpreter, or perhaps by nonverbal signs such as gesture or pictorial symbol that appeal to the experience of the person being addressed.

The process of unification is characteristic of all personal development. The task of forging a personal identity has been dramatically portrayed by psychologists and by philosophical and literary existentialists in the recent past. The understanding of meaning as the search for one's self, the choice and appropriation of an identity, has been central among the images that have shaped the generations of the twentieth century. But the dramatic emphasis that has been placed on the hero and on the moment of crisis by the literature of existentialism may obscure the fact that personal development is often more mundane than one might suppose from portrayals of Orestes, Lear, or Sisyphus.

The issue can be stated quite simply. I am a son, husband, lover, friend, competitor, citizen, colleague, and teacher. Each of these identities, which operate on different levels, contributes to my sense of myself. Sometimes they complement one another and at other times they conflict. My duty as a husband may conflict with my vocation as teacher or scholar. Similarly, the roles of friend and citizen may come into conflict. In every moment I forge an identity that integrates or pulls together all of these different roles into a sense of myself as a person. I think, I act, other persons respond to me, and I respond to their responses. I am a romantic and a moralist, and sometimes these are in tension. If the tension between any of these roles should become exacerbated to the point at which integration was impossible, if two or more identities in which I participate were totally irreconcilable, then schizophrenia would result. Short of that there is a huge array of defenses, including deceit and compartmentalization, that may allow me to appear in contradictory roles to different audiences both within and without myself. Each decision and action involves, however, a provisional kind of integration. This kind of integration or unification is always present in the growth and development of the self. Theology and religion have often provided imaginative expression for this integration. Such notions as destiny, vocation, divine good pleasure, *karma*, and the will of God are ways of expressing a kind of unity of the self in relation to its world.[6]

It is an implication of the position defended in this study that selfhood is not a primitive concept or a datum of our experience. We are led to the idea of the self in order to account for the subjective unity of our experience. The idea by which we represent this subjective unity to ourselves, however, varies considerably in the course of the development of an individual, as it varies across cultures and historical epochs. Just as conceptions of *God*, a term closely associated with the unity of our experience (e.g., Creator, redeemer, kingdom of God), vary across cultures and among persons, conceptions of the *self*, a term that represents the subjective unity of our experience, will show a similar variation. If one held that the self was a datum that was available directly in experience to all selves, there would be no reason to expect such variation or to imagine that diverse conceptions of the self would fall into several types.

THE TYPOLOGY

The term *type* is here being employed to signify a construction of elements that have been abstracted from specific doctrines or systems of thought and used to form a coherent and consistent pattern that might shed further light on the work from which the elements were abstracted. This usage is indebted to Max Weber's development of the concept of *ideal type*.[7] A type is a model constructed from a set of particular instances in order to generalize about those instances. The process of abstraction involves exaggeration and idealization in order to construct a model that is consistent and coherent. In employing such a procedure, one incurs the risk of creating stereotypes and caricatures that can be dealt with more easily than the actual material being analyzed. The advantage of such a procedure, however, is that the construction of consistent and coherent models may serve to illumine the systems of thought that are under analysis, and to reveal implications that had hitherto gone unnoticed.

Three different conceptions of the unity of the self and its relation to monotheism will be considered. Each of these involves a different typical conception of the status of the finite in relation to the infinite.

The *monistic* conception is one in which the fundamental unit is the whole. The finite has no integrity of its own. It gains significance as part of the whole in which it participates. Often the finite individual is conceived as participating in but ignorant of or estranged from its infinite source, to which it unconsciously longs to return. The principle of individuation is not identical with God or being. It is rather an alien influence that contributes to fragmentation and estrangement. The vision of God or the attainment of the highest good involves the return of the individual to the unity of the whole.

The situation of the finite individual is one of estrangement and is therefore essentially tragic. Estrangement represents a separation from a natural union previously enjoyed. Two discrete individuals may have had no opportunity for intercourse, but they are not estranged. The term refers to a state of separation in what was previously a harmonious relation. The word *ignorance* used above might be more accurately replaced by the Platonic term *anamnesis*, which suggests that a prior knowledge or awareness can be recollected. The finite individual is estranged from its ground and is thus incomplete or distorted. It possesses no integrity.

Knowledge occurs when the knower participates in that which is known. Ideally, there is no separation between being and knowing in this conception. To know God is to become God. The interpretation of language as a system or even an aggregate of symbols is characteristic of this type. A symbol participates in the reality that it discloses. Knowing is a form of participation.

The motif of return is central to this conception. The end of life is the overcoming of estrangement, the striving for a union that may be approached but that can never be achieved within the structures of finitude. This struggle for union between knower and known, lover and beloved, is eros. Ecstasy is that moment in the life of the mystic when he stands outside of himself and achieves momentary union with the cosmos. But these are only moments or components of experience. Final fulfillment can be projected only into the past (Plato's *anamnesis* or the mythology of Eden) or into the future (the kingdom of God).

The *individualistic* conception is one in which individual finite substance has its own integrity . Nothing essential is lacking to it. Finite individuals are the basic constituents of reality. The world is the totality of individuals, of facts, or substances. This does not mean that the individual is not dependent upon God or the infinite for its existence. It is, however, an entity.

The finite individual is portrayed primarily as will, or as agent. Since the nominalism of late medieval philosophy, and since the writings of Descartes, individual substance has been conceived primarily as will.[8] The autonomy of the individual is stressed. In some existentialist writing this emphasis on autonomy borders on the isolation of the individual. Thinking, willing, and remembering are activities of the self. They are not to be interpreted as participation in

God's thinking, willing, and remembering. Decision and judgment are prominent in the individual's exercise of his autonomy.

The fact that no ontological estrangement is implied in this conception does not mean that suffering is not taken seriously. Rather, it is interpreted differently. The notion of moral drama is more appropriate to this conception than is the notion of tragedy. The world is composed of individuals, finite and infinite, and therefore the powers of good and the powers of evil are ascribed to individuals. God and the devil are personifications of powers within whose fields of influence men operate. Individuals initiate acts and are acted upon. They are never able to enter one another or to participate in the being of one another. They attract, repel, collide, and cooperate.

Knowledge of self is primary. The self is held to have private access to its own thoughts, deliberations, and feelings that is unavailable to any other individual. On the basis of this certain touchstone, the self builds its knowledge of the world and of God. *Cogito ergo sum.* The self is the original datum.

The goal of life is conceived in terms appropriate to individual perfection. It is the fulfillment of duty, the life lived authentically, or the justification of the individual. History is composed of a series of moments in which decisions are made and events occur. It is less a process than a series of individual moments.

The *social* conception is that in which a notion of community or society is taken to be fundamental. A person is a system of social relations as well as an individual entity. Relations are not external or accidental. They are intrinsic to the development and the constitution of each individual. The metaphor of the *polis* can be applied to individuals as well as to the whole. Being is social.

This conception arose out of an awareness of social and cultural interdependence. Systems of metaphysics that have expressed this social conception of reality have developed since the early nineteenth century. The organic metaphor of the romantics was combined with new discoveries of developmental processes in nature and in society. The rise of the social sciences has accompanied the development of this conception of reality.

The development of an individual is a process that takes time. The individual emerges by differentiating himself from others and creating his own personal identity in the context of the social and natural orders. Time is an essential constituent of the metaphysical system. The monistic and individualistic types are finally atemporal. Participation of the part in the whole and the immediate encounter between individuals are not temporal processes. The development of the individual, however, is mediated by events that occur in time, by language, and by the entire context of social and cultural relations.

Knowledge is mediated. Language, memory, and social interaction influence perception and conception. Knowing occurs by comparison and judgment. Interpretation involves comparison, and judgment takes time. It is a process of mediation. There is no unmediated intuition. The self is not a datum. A person's understanding of his own individuality is conditioned and mediated by the language and actions of others. This understanding is an interpretation of who he is in the light of what he remembers of who he was and the hopes and fears he has for the future. Time and discourse are essential to such understanding.

The individual is not deficient in being. His goal is not reunion with the whole and extinction of his individual existence. It is expansion through multiple relations and harmony with all individuals and with God. The goal of an individual life as well as the goal of the race is community. In community individuals are united while they retain their individuality.

These typical conceptions may be viewed as a schematization of different ways of resolving the classical problem of the relation between the one and the many. In the monistic conception, the fact of plurality is questioned. Plurality is to be explained as a modification of that which is one substance. In the individualistic conception, plurality is recognized. There are many substances. Individuals have their own integrity. In the social conception, reality is an interpretation and harmony of many individuals. The whole is not an aggregate because individuals have no existence apart from others, and yet the category of individual or finite substance is retained.

EXPRESSIVE AND DESCRIPTIVE ADEQUACY

It is a contention of this study that the monistic and individualistic conceptions are both abstractions from a third and more comprehensive type of philosophy of religion. Each results from a selective focus on particular aspects of human experience that have been abstracted from the social character of that experience. The typology is employed here in the service of two tasks. The first presents each of the types and notes the aspects of experience that are most salient in it. The second evaluates the adequacy of each of these types.

A preliminary distinction may be drawn between expressive and descriptive adequacy. A vision or conception may be expressively adequate in that it provides a lucid and reliable account of certain aspects of experience, but it might be judged descriptively inadequate if the account that it provides is irreconcilable with some aspect of our knowledge of ourselves and our world. The three types may properly be viewed as expressions of different aspects of human experience. The monistic type grows out of and expresses an experience, associated with the major mystical traditions of East and West, in which boundaries are felt to be relative and to give way to an undifferentiated unity of the whole. It is correlated with the experience of unity with the cosmos or with the ground of all being, and is grounded in the experience of unbounded trust. The individualistic type conveys the experience of claim, or the sense of something or someone standing over against the self. Whether the claim be that of another person, of moral and aesthetic values, or of God, the experience is one of distance between the self and the other. The social type is rooted in the experiences of frustrated and broken relationships, and of creative growth. It is an expression of the attempt to forge social relationships and community out of the various roles in which the self is engaged. The experience of trust and unity, the force of the claims of others and the conflict produced by those claims, and the successes and frustrations of social relationships are shared by all persons. At different points in the life of a person or a community, however, one of these aspects is more salient than the others.

The types can be evaluated according to the adequacy of their expression of each of these aspects of experience. It might be argued, for instance, that Spinoza's *Ethics* is a more sensitive presentation of the experience of trust in a unity that undergirds all being and power than is Brown's *Love's Body*.[9] Spinoza, however, if not Brown, intends his work to be more than an expression of aspects of experience that are particularly characteristic of him or of his culture. He intends to construct a model that provides an adequate description of the world.

The experience of alienation, or of isolation bordering on solipsism, is characteristic of some moments in the lives of most persons, and is more pronounced for some than for others. A philosophical or theological work may portray such an experience with aesthetic and analytic power. That would not, however, be sufficient ground for its adoption as the basis of a metaphysical scheme. Such an experience is not sufficiently comprehensive to provide an interpretation of the variety of social and cultural experience. The study of languages, of social interaction, of the development of cognition and affect, provides evidence that human life is social, that the self is a social construct, and that the experience of radical isolation is inadequate as a comprehensive description of the relation of the self to its social environment. Within a conceptual framework of the social type, however, it is possible to comprehend and interpret experiences of mystical union and those of radical isolation.

Each of the three types is adequate for the expression of particular aspects of human experience, but only the third is sufficiently comprehensive to provide the basis for an adequate philosophical description of the self and its world, and thus for an adequate conception of God. The monistic and individualistic types are expressive of moments in the religious consciousness, but when they are elevated into fundamental philosophical categories they yield implications that are belied by our knowledge of the social character of human language and activity. The vision of monistic union suggests that experiences between selves, and boundaries between conflicting bodies and wills, may finally be transcended. The individualistic type suggests isolated personal identity as a touchstone for epistemological and ethical issues. Both are aspects of human experience, but neither is sufficiently comprehensive. The first two types can best be understood as abstractions from the social type. As such, they are less adequate than the third type for a descriptive account of the structure of self and world.

Contemporary investigations of the concept of the self point to the greater adequacy of the social type. Self-awareness is not a primitive datum. Rather, it is the consequence of a sophisticated development and differentiation in a social and temporal context. Mead described the development of the self as the increasing differentiation of subjective and objective awareness in the "I" and the "me."[10] Others have offered similar analyses of the development of self-awareness through the acquisition and differentiation of linguistic skills and social roles.[11]

Much work in the social sciences during the last several decades has revealed a close relationship between ontogenetic and phylogenetic development.[12] Similar patterns of evolution and sequential stages have been discerned in the lives of individuals, of groups, and of entire cultures. The basic structure of these patterns is that of increasing differentiation, followed by reintegration that results in a more complex unity.

An example of the way in which the distinction between the several conceptions of God and the self developed here could be related to study of the development of persons in society is provided by parallels between the types and the stages of development described by Erik Erikson.[13] Erikson describes the initial stage of the human life cycle as one in which the primary issue is that of basic trust.[14] An infant is comfortable and at home in the arms of its mother, afraid and estranged elsewhere. The first issue to be resolved is for the infant to begin to trust the warmth and love of the mother (and thus of the world) even in moments of physical separation. This trust that love and care will endure, that the universe is fundamentally benevolent, is the message proclaimed by Paul Tillich when he says "You are accepted."[15] The establishment of trust on this global level is essential for further development of the individual. Love and care endure even in the absence of immediate contact. If trust is not firmly established in the relation between infant and mother, it remains an unresolved, though perhaps unconscious, issue in the life of the individual.

The infant next comes to realize that it can affect its environment. A sense of will or autonomy dawns.[16] The child learns that it can achieve results by smiling or crying. It discovers and experiments with its own body as distinct from that of its mother. This distinctness does not mean undifferentiated estrangement and homelessness. Rather, it enters into the development of a sense of "me" and "mine." Earlier the child was afraid of estrangement from the mother and desired to be reunited with her, but now it is afraid of being swallowed up by her and of being unable to establish its own autonomy. As it experiments with its ability to initiate, it is important that it establish itself as a person in its own right, and not be devoured into the whole. The development of autonomy is aided by identification with the other parent. This is the triadic situation described by Freud's employment of the Oedipus myth. The child identifies with the father as a way of establishing its individuality over against the threat of absorption into the mother.[17] By means of this identification autonomy is initially secured. The struggle for autonomy continues throughout adolescence and through the stage Erikson has described as an identity crisis, during which the choice of vocational and social roles is crucial.[18]

Following the development of the autonomous self, the need continually to stand over against one's environment is relaxed, and a search begins for new relationships and new forms of community. The relevant danger now is not the threat of being absorbed by parent or family, but isolation. Children's play, sharing, and the choices of school, of career, and of intimate relationships that endure are part of achieving a new sociality for the differentiated ego. Associations are not ascribed, as was the early family life, but arise out of choices to enter freely into new forms of relationship. The generation of a family and the facing of issues of meaning and of the purpose of one's life within the context of communal responsibility involve acceptance of oneself as a social being, an acceptance that is possible only after the autonomy of the individual self has been secured.

These stages are not bound to specific chronological periods. Certainly they overlap. Play between children contains the beginning of social peer relationships, while the development of a sense of autonomy continues through adolescence. It is the sequence that is important, and the formation of new, more complex forms of relationship through the process of differentiation and autonomy.

The issues expressed by the monistic, individualistic, and social types are paralleled by the stages in the course of human development. Each of the issues that arise during the early stages of development remains basic to mature life. To relate these issues to stages in the process of the evolution of consciousness is not to detract from their enduring importance. Issues of trust, autonomy, authority, and the creation of social bonds are present in the life of every individual and group. Such parallels aid in interpreting the fact that different issues and paradigms grasp and are grasped by persons, societies, and cultures at different stages in their histories.

Similar stages have been observed in the life of groups.[19] To one entering a room filled with strangers, a group appears as an undifferentiated mass. Persons are reluctant to individuate themselves by stepping out from the anonymity of the mass. They respond to each other on the basis of stereotypes of dress, tone of voice, vocabulary, or past associations. Some individuals adopt leadership roles and others identify or enter into conflict with the leader as a means of differentiation and the establishment of autonomy. As the members gain autonomy and the ability to initiate, they begin to share common experiences and to develop a conscious sense of community. Historical parallels show similar sequential development in other social and cultural institutions. Contemporary social theorists have presented a wealth of illustrative material illuminating this developmental process.[20] In each case, the sequence is from an undifferentiated monistic state, to the establishment of autonomy through a focus on the will and on the ability to initiate and choose, to the development of new and more intimate forms of association and community.

In order to provide illustrations of the types, three authors have been selected whose works represent contemporary alternatives in philosophical theology. Paul Tillich was one of the most influential philosophical theologians of this century. His *Systematic Theology* (1951-1963) presents an articulation of the basic philosophical questions of human existence and a correlation with these questions of answers revealed by God in Jesus as the Christ. One of Tillich's most influential modes of teaching and writing involved the construction of typologies to illustrate the history of an idea, the development of a culture, or the place of a work of art within a particular cultural epoch. He was aware of his own positions in the light of alternative options. Although Tillich perceived his work as a synthesis of the conceptions under investigation, the analysis in the following chapter will demonstrate that his affinity is with the monistic and mystical tradition. This affinity is rooted in his early work on Schelling and Jakob Böhme and it continues to inform his thought throughout the *Systematic Theology*. Tillich continues the Platonic and monistic tradition even while he provides further differentiation within that tradition in order to account for aspects of experience that have been more clearly illumined by other models.

Austin Farrer was a theologian of the Church of England, and professor of philosophical theology at Oxford. Farrer was little known outside the Anglican communion. He was as parochial in his writing and theological style as Tillich was cosmopolitan. But Farrer was also a highly imaginative thinker. He turned to poetry, to the use of symbols in biblical and other myths, and to careful examination of the language that men employ to describe their experience. Farrer concentrated his attention on the activity of the imagination in knowing and choosing. The spectrum of free human activity, which extends from conscious volitional choice to the poetic use of the imagination, provided material for his analysis of man. This analysis served as the clue to finite substance generally and provided analogies for Farrer to describe the apprehension of infinite substance, or God.

Josiah Royce is the only one of the figures to be considered who was not a professional theologian. He considered the elaboration of a concept of God to lie within the scope of philosophy as a part of the task of describing and accounting for what is. Royce's discussion of the role of community in the development of the self and of the way in which membership in the human community is essential

34 GOD AND THE SELF

even in contexts where men are thought to be independent or isolated is crucial to the third type. His use of Charles Peirce's theory of cognition as interpretation and his discussion of the community of interpretation provide the recognition of social and temporal mediation in knowing that is fundamental to the social type. Royce's discussion of the beloved community and its philosophical and theological implications is most fully set forth in *The Problem of Christianity* (1913), which will be the focus of the discussion in chapter 4.

NOTES

1. Clifford Geertz, *The Interpretation of Cultures* (New York: Basic Books, 1973), p. 93.

2. The work of Mircea Eliade, who has been the most influential theorist of religion in this country since the Second World War, represents an interpretation of archaic religion as an attractive option, engendering nostalgia for an immediate relation to the cosmos, which has been lost. In the foreword to what he considers to be the most significant of his books, Eliade notes that the Judeo-Christian emphasis on history has led to Marxism, historicism, and existentialism. He might also have said that Western culture has led to World War II. This essay, first published in 1949, is an eloquent appeal for a return to an immediate unity with the cosmos that is attributed to archaic man, though Eliade finally acknowledges that such a return is not possible. It was through this essay that Eliade's work became popular among students of religion in the 1950s. See Mircea Eliade, *Cosmos and History: The Myth of the Eternal Return*, trans. W. R. Trask, (New York: Harper and Row, 1959), p. xi.

3. For a discussion of interpretations of the *imago dei* in the writings of Irenaeus, Clement of Alexandria, Athanasius, and others, see David Cairns, *The Image of God in Man* (London: Student Christian Movement Press, 1953).

4. John Calvin, *Institutes of the Christian Religion*, ed., J. McNeill, trans. F. Battles, (Philadelphia: The Westminster Press, 1960), p. 35.

5. Immanuel Kant, *Critique of Pure Reason*, ed. and trans. N. K. Smith, (London: Macmillan and Company, 1933), pp. 242–52, 328–83.

6. Recent revival of interest in the I Ching, astrology, and tarot cards may represent an attempt to discover unity in external controls by a generation and a society in which the confusion of roles and the difficulty of grasping the unity of the self has become nearly unbearable for some. See Philip Slater, *The Pursuit of Loneliness: American Culture at the Breaking Point* (Boston: Beacon Press, 1970).

7. For a discussion of Weber's use of ideal type, see Max Weber, *The Methodology of the Social Sciences*, trans. E. A. Shils and H. A. Finch (New York: The Free Press of Glencoe, 1949), chap. 2; and Talcott Parsons, *The Structure of Social Action* (New York: The Free Press, 1968), 2: 601–10.

8. A fundamental voluntarism pervades Cartesian thought. The act of the self doubting, and thinking about itself doubting, is the locus of the intuition of the self. More significant, however, is the fact that Descartes invokes the creative activity of God at each moment to guarantee such order as we discover in

mathematical truths, and to relate *res cogitans* and *res extensa.* A voluntaristic conception of the deity underlies all structures. See Robert Neville, "Some Historical Problems about the Transcendence of God," *The Journal of Religion* 47 (1967): 1–9.

9. Benedict de Spinoza, "Ethics," in *Works of Spinoza,* V. 2 trans. R. H. Elwes, (New York: Dover, 1951); Norman O. Brown, *Love's Body* (New York: Random House, 1966).

10. George Herbert Mead, *Mind, Self and Society* (Chicago: University of Chicago Press, 1934).

11. Theodore R. Sarbin, "A Preface to a Psychological Analysis of the Self," *Psychological Review* 59 (1952): 11–22; Gordon W. Allport, *Becoming* (New Haven, Conn.: Yale University Press, 1954); Erving Goffman, *The Presentation of Self in Everyday Life* (New York: Doubleday, 1959); Shelley Duval and Robert A. Wicklund, *A Theory of Objective Self-Awareness* (New York: Academic Press, 1972).

12. See, for example, Robert N. Bellah, "Religious Evolution," *Beyond Belief* (New York: Harper and Row, 1970), pp. 20–50; Erik Erikson, *Childhood and Society* (New York: W. W. Norton and Company, 1963); Erich Neumann, *The Origins and History of Consciousness,* trans. R.F.C. Hull, (New York: Pantheon, 1954); Philip Slater, *Microcosm* (New York: Wiley, 1966); and Peter Wolff, "The Developmental Psychologies of Jean Piaget and Psychoanalysis," *Psychological Issues,* 2, no. 1 (New York: International Universities Press, 1960).

13. Erikson, *Childhood and Society,* pp. 247–74.

14. Ibid., pp. 247–51.

15. Tillich's phrase, "Accept the fact that you are accepted," suggests a self-consciousness that is inclusive of another stage. It is an invitation to actively appropriate one's own existence. Paul Tillich, "You are Accepted," *The Shaking of the Foundations* (New York: Charles Scribner's Sons, 1959), p. 162.

16. Erikson, *Childhood and Society,* pp. 251–54.

17. Philip Slater, "Toward a Dualistic Theory of Identification," *Merrill-Palmer Quarterly* 7 (1961): 113–26.

18. Erikson, *Childhood and Society,* pp. 261–63.

19. Slater, *Microcosm,* pp. 234–52.

20. See n12 above.

2

The Centered Self: The Monistic Type

The consideration of the work of Paul Tillich as an example of the monistic type is a controversial one. Tillich would undoubtedly resist such a label. In this chapter I shall argue that Tillich's discussions of the self and God are set in the context of an essential monism. It could be argued that no dialectical thinker can be simply categorized as monistic, and thus it would be advisable to choose another example that more clearly exemplifies the type.

There are good reasons for choosing Tillich, however. An aim of this study is to demonstrate the possibility of grouping viable conceptions of God and the self in a manner that reveals the aspects of experience that are highlighted by each, and to which each appeals. Tillich has had an influence equal to and perhaps greater than that of any other American theologian in this century. This influence has not been confined to theologians and philosophers, but has extended to members of many academic disciplines. Furthermore, Tillich is a contemporary spokesman for a Platonic tradition in philosophy and theology that provides expression for the mystical aspects of human experience and that dramatizes a basic trust in the unity of all being and knowing. This tradition must be represented in any consideration of contemporary options. It is more appropriate, then, to show that the monistic vision governs Tillich's work and the experience to which he appeals than it would be to analyze the work of a less influential thinker who might exemplify a more obviously monistic metaphysics.

The selective character of the following analysis may appear to be more capricious in relation to Tillich's thought than in the cases of Farrer and Royce. The *Systematic Theology* has a very definite structure, but that structure does not define a linear argument in the manner of the works of Farrer and Royce that are being considered here. The method of correlation between existential question and theological answer is at work in each part of the system. It is a method that frees Tillich to structure his exposition according to the traditional order, which follows the tripartite division of the Apostle's Creed into sections dealing with God the Father, God the Son, and God the Holy Spirit. To this core Tillich adds an introductory part dealing with reason and revelation, and a concluding part on history and the kingdom of God. But the order of the *Systematic Theology* does not define the order of an argument as do Austin Farrer's *Finite and Infinite* and Josiah Royce's *The Problem of Christianity*. Thus selections have been chosen from those passages in Tillich's writings which bear most directly on his treatment of the relation between finite and infinite and the unity of the self.

THE TYPE

The problems of the one and the many, of monism and dualism, of eternity and time, are among the central issues in Tillich's writing. How does the conditioned participate in the unconditioned? What is the relation between finite and infinite? How is faith to be distinguished from idolatry or finite concerns from ultimate concern? Tillich stressed repeatedly his intention to render a faithful account of the tension between the conditioned and the unconditioned and not to lose the polarities of experience in a metaphysics of idealism. Though he recognized the issues and attempted to maintain the tension, the monistic alternative is most pronounced in his work. His analysis of the alternatives and his own preference are evident in an article published in 1946 under the title "The Two Types of Philosophy of Religion." The first two paragraphs of that article make his position clear.

> One can distinguish two ways of approaching God: the way of overcoming estrangement and the way of meeting a stranger. In the first way man discovers *himself* when he discovers God; he discovers something that is identical with himself although it transcends him infinitely, something from which he is estranged, but from which he never has been and never can be separated. In the second way man meets a *stranger* when he meets God. The meeting is accidental. Essentially they do not belong to each other. They may become friends on a tentative and conjectural basis. But there is no certainty about the stranger man has met. He may disappear, and only *probable* statements can be made about his nature.
>
> The two ways symbolize the two possible types of philosophy of religion: the ontological type and the cosmological type. The way of overcoming estrangement symbolizes the ontological method in the philosophy of religion. The way of meeting a stranger symbolizes the cosmological method. It is the purpose of this essay to show: (1) that the ontological method is basic for every philosophy of religion, (2) that the cosmological method without the ontological as its basis leads to a destructive cleavage between philosophy and religion, and (3) that on the basis of the ontological approach with a dependent use of the cosmological way, philosophy of religion contributes to a reconciliation between religion and secular culture.[1]

I shall argue that Tillich's two types are both abstractions from a third, and more comprehensive, type of philosophy of religion. Both the ontological and cosmological approaches result from the selective focus on particular aspects of human experience that have been abstracted from the social character of that experience. This third approach will be considered below in the chapter on the social type. It is clear, though, from the above quotation that Tillich is affirming the ontological way.

According to the ontological way, when man discovers God he discovers himself. God is the prius of all knowing. Knowledge of God cannot be inferred by amassing data and presenting arguments. It is immediate. A Socratic method of questioning is appropriate for the teaching of theology. That which is sought is already present in the possibility of the question, or in the possibility of *any* question. The fact that the cosmological method, the way of meeting a stranger, can provide no certainty, is regarded by Tillich as an inadequacy of that method. One is never certain of the identity of the other. The mark of the ontological method is that it does provide certainty. Knowledge is immediate. Judgment concerning the adequacy of the knowledge is unnecesssary. The ideal instance of knowing is one in which the knower participates in the known and the relation between them is immediate.

Ontology. Tillich interprets the conditions of existence as a state of alienation or estrangement from the ground to which the finite individual rightfully belongs. The estrangement or alienation of finite existence from the divine life, and the manifestation of that estrangement in anxiety, provide the point from which Tillich's analysis of the relation between finite and infinite begins. The experience of anxiety or estrangement, and the contrasting ecstatic participation in the ground of all being, inform all of Tillich's work.

The ontological structure is characterized by polarities, the chief of which is the polarity of self and world. It is within this polarity that the existential situation of man is set. The conditions of life are elaborated by Tillich in a four-level ontological analysis.[2] The first level is that of the relation between self and world; the second consists of three pairs of polar elements (individualization and participation, dynamics and form, freedom and destiny); the third expresses the difference between essential and existential being; and the fourth deals with the basic forms of thought and being, traditionally called the categories (time, space, cause, substance). Each of these structures is a priori, in the sense that it is a necessary condition of all of our experience.

After describing the conditions of finite existence, Tillich suggests that we experience a power, a ground that is unconditioned. Ontological analysis and the raising of existential questions can lead to a sense of power and of mystery that is not exhausted by the categories or elements specified in the ontological analysis. This unconditional element is not something that is experienced apart from the self-world structure of reality, the polar elements, the conditions of existence, or the categories of knowing and being. Rather, it is experienced through them, but it is not exhausted by them. It is this unconditioned element that Tillich refers to as being, or the power or ground of being. When the Unconditioned is the object of our ultimate concern, it can be referred to as God.

The polarities and conditions of existence are overcome in the divine life, or in being-itself. Tillich affirms the Platonic notion that being is one, and that the conditions of finite existence involve a fragmentation of that unity. Finitude is characterized by the split between essence and existence, while God enjoys the perfection of unity:

> He is beyond the split. But the universe is subject to the split. God alone is "perfect," a word which is exactly defined as being beyond the gap between essential and existential being. Man and his world do not have this perfection. Their existence stands out of their essence as in a "fall." On this point the Platonic and the Christian evaluations of existence coincide.[3]

Interpreters of Tillich have been correct in rejecting a simple monism. Tillich's dialectical thought contains a dynamism at its core. The basic vision, though, and the aspect of experience that is expressed by the ontology is a vision or experience of a power, a unity, a ground that is manifest in, but never exhausts itself in, the beings, events, thoughts, and actions of the finite order. James Luther Adams relates it both to the Logos of Greek speculation and to the monotheism of the Jewish-Christian tradition.

> The concept of the Unconditioned, as the ultimate that is presupposed by all meaning, being, and value (conditioning and supporting them), is a composite concept. In Tillich's usage it draws upon and modifies the ontological and axiological concepts of Greek and modern thought, from Anaximander and Parmenides to Spinoza and Kant, though in its modified form it aims to give expression to the Jewish-Christian idea of the majesty and unspeakable richness of the divine.[4]

Its most recent roots are in Böhme and Schelling, both of whom combined the mystic's appreciation of a unity that underlies all with a rejection of the static notion of being that is often associated with monistic and idealistic metaphysics.

The unconditioned elements in our experience point to the depth of that experience, beyond the ontological structures and even beyond the fundamental polarity of self and world. Tillich employs the notion of *ground* to recall aspects of experience such as the depth of the ocean with its mythological and psychological connotations, the depth that is discovered upon further investigation of a phenomenon known only superficially, and the depth of despair. These images do not exclude the personal. It is possible to speak of the depth of personal existence and of interpersonal relationships. But these images do transcend the personal.

> "Personal God" does not mean that God is *a* person. It means that God is the ground of everything personal and that he carries within himself the ontological power of personality. . . . God became "a person" only in the nineteenth century, in connection with the Kantian separation of nature ruled by physical law from personality ruled by moral law.[5]

The notion of person is rather recent, though the separation that Tillich describes can be traced back at least to Luther and to late medieval nominalism. Tillich tried to transcend this notion by interpreting the development of the person within the structures of existence and by affirming an undifferentiated ground of being as the context of those structures. He constantly cautions against reifying this ground. It lies beyond all linguistic and experiential distinctions. It must be beyond, because every object and distinction is presented within experience, and the power of being provides the ground for that experience.

Epistemology. Knowing is achieved through participation. The finite participates in the infinite. The knower participates in the object of his knowing. Knowing is interpreted as a form of recollection. The knower is not alien from the object he seeks to know, but is distanced from that object through estrangement and deficiency. In order to know the object he must reunite himself with the being of that object. The same theme is present in Plato's employment of the analogies of the cave and of the divided line and in the Plotinian chain of being. Distance from the source or power of being is a measure of deficiency in being. At the outer extremity participation is reduced and knowledge is lessened correspondingly.

An implication of this way of conceiving knowing is that knowledge is equated with power or being. To know something is to participate in it, or to be that thing. To know God is to participate in the being of God or to participate in God's knowing himself.

> We *know* because we participate in the divine knowledge. Truth is not absolutely removed from the outreach of our finite minds, since the divine life in which we are rooted embodies all truth.[6]

Tillich speaks of the "depth" character of all knowledge because knowing participates in the ground and the power of being. Knowledge cannot take place at a distance. It involves becoming one with the object known.[7]

This manner of conceiving man's knowledge of God is related to the use of the ontological idea. Since to know God is to participate in the ground of being, and all beings participate in this ground to varying degrees, then all beings have some, perhaps inchoate, knowledge of God. Though Tillich objects to the ontological argument as an argument, he understands it to have a valid function as a "description of the way in which infinity is present in actual finitude."[8] It is this presence of infinity in finitude and finitude in infinity that is the participation that constitutes knowledge. God is the first "object" of knowing. But God is properly not an "object" at all; he is the ground of all knowing and is therefore prior to, and presupposed in, all knowledge.

Doubt is never finally threatening. Faith includes an element of immediate awareness that provides certainty in the ontological approach. Doubt is always present in faith, but it is the inverse side of the same faith. Thus doubt itself functions as evidence that the prius of all thinking and doubting is God.

> If doubt appears, it should not be considered as the negation of faith, but as an element which was always and will always be present in the act of faith.[9]

Any experience of distance or of differentiation within the context of the monistic type carries with it the assurance that there exists a whole from which one is estranged and an interest in overcoming that estrangement through reunion.

> The profundity of the term "estrangement" lies in the implication that one belongs essentially to that from which one is estranged.[10]

Doubt is interpreted as a struggle that witnesses to (1) an

interest in overcoming that doubt and eliminating the struggle, and (2) a fulfillment of that interest.

Ethics. Tillich employs two different images to describe sin: estrangement and idolatry. Estrangement constitutes his interpretation of the doctrine of original sin. The existential situation of the finite individual is one in which it is estranged from the ground of its being. The doctrine of original sin is translated into such terms as estrangement and anxiety. The second image, idolatry, refers not to the truth behind original sin, but rather to the doctrine of actual or active sin. Men often direct their loyalties toward ends that are not God. They attempt to elevate the private, the parochial, the idolatrous into an object of ultimate concern.

A metaphysical model based on an undifferentiated whole allows of no way to imagine or to express distance across which knowledge or action may take place. That is to say, it allows of no way to express empty space, or distances between discrete entities. Distance in the monistic context is always conceived within a plenum, within the context of the unity of being. Time and space are categorial structures of the existential condition, which are set within the larger ontological whole. Space is a category of being under the conditions of existence. Therefore, the unity of being is more fundamental than the distances between beings. This contrasts with the individualistic type, in which the universe is conceived as an aggregate of discrete individuals rather than as a plenum. In this first type, distance can only be conceived within the unity of being, which ultimately transcends all boundaries and all spaces. It is impossible, then, to conceive of empty space between beings. Distance is always measured in degrees of participation and estrangement. Distance is overcome, both epistemologically and ontologically, by increased participation of the part in the whole. Again, this contrasts with the individualistic type, where distance is overcome through the meeting or encounter of two individuals.

The experience of moral claim, of something that ought to be done, is an experience that phenomenologically suggests distance. It is the distance or discrepancy between what is and what ought to be. In order to do justice to this basic experience of moral claim, Tillich must discover a way of representing ethical distance or judgment. Within the monistic context of this first type, the experience of claim or over-againstness is expressed by the invocation of the expansive and universal to criticize the private, parochial, and idolatrous. The paradigm of sin is the attempt to place ultimate concern and allegiance in an object that is not ultimate, or to elevate a finite good to the highest good. The only proper object of ultimate concern is God, or being-itself. When God is made the object of concern, all of the parts of the whole will be objects according to their proper places. They will be objects of concern to the extent to which they participate in the depth structure of human existence. This is in accord with traditional hierarchies of value. The highest good also includes the proper ordering of other goods. To have regard for the ground of being is also to have regard for the harmonious relation of all finite beings.

Tillich follows Augustine in his interpretation of the command to love the neighbor as a command to love the neighbor as a creature of God. It is the God-createdness which makes the creature lovable. A value is affirmed because it participates in the depth of being. The individual person or object does not possess intrinsic value in itself, but it is valuable insofar as it participates in the ground of being, or in God. Proper self-love is loving the infinite in oneself. Human love of God and human self-love are both identical with and involve participation in God's love of himself.

It has been said that man's love of God is the love with which God loves himself. This is an expression of the truth that God is a subject even where he seems to be an object. It points directly to a divine self-love and indirectly, by analogy, to a divinely demanded human self-love. . . .

This makes it possible also to apply the term agape to the love wherein man loves himself, that is, himself as the eternal image in the divine life. . . .

The divine self-love includes all creatures; and proper human self-love includes everything with which man is existentially united. (1:282)

In these descriptions of divine and human love, as in the earlier discussion of knowledge, there is no distance between subject and object. Participation does not allow for distance. Epistemology and ethics exemplify the same pattern.

Salvation is understood to be the reunion of the self with the ground of its being. Tillich stresses the notion of eros as the drive for this reunion. The reunion is reconciliation. It is the foundation of love.

Every individual, since he is separated from the whole, desires reunion with the whole. His "poverty" makes him seek for abundance. This is the root of love in all of its forms. (2:52)

This reunion is restoration to a state prior (to use a temporal metaphor) to finitude and existential alienation. To accept the fact that one is accepted is to accept the reality of union with the ground of one's being even in the state of partial estrangement. The saint is one who is reconciled with God and who therefore shares in his being and glory. It is a view of salvation as restoration and reconciliation that differs from interpretations that stress either the justification of the individual or sanctification where both God and the saints increase in glory.

The Tillichian interpretation of distance as estrangement and alienation has proved suitable for describing much contemporary experience, as Tillich showed so effectively in *The Courage to Be*. Estrangement, alienation, and sin are identified with anxiety, restlessness, and the experience of meaningless and are employed to interpret the need for unity and meaning in a culture that is in conflict with itself. This first type provides expression for these feelings of estrangement and alienation as well as for their polar opposites, such as the mystic's sense of oneness with the universe, the infant's sense of trust in the world of the mother, or the basic sense of comfort in the world. The negative and positive sides of this cluster of feelings are contrast-dependent. The feeling of estrangement and the idealization of a state of reunion and lack of differentiation appear together.

THE STRUCTURE OF BEING

Each of the five parts of Tillich's *Systematic Theology* opens with a question posed by human experience and juxtaposes with this question an answer provided by theology on the basis of the revelation in Jesus as the Christ. This juxtaposition is Tillich's method of correlation. Men are driven to the depths of existence and to questions that cannot be answered from within the subject-object structure. The question of God is the question of the whole. Why is there something rather than nothing? It is the question of the origin of all things (birth) and of the end (death). It is the question that demands an account of the conditions within which all other questions are asked and answered. Under the rubric "Being and the Question of God" at the outset of the second part of the *Systematic Theology,* Tillich sets forth his basic ontological structure. The following commentary on some passages of that text will focus on Tillich's description of the polarity of self and world in relation to the question of being.

Reason is subordinate to being. The relation is one of participation:

Like everything else, reason has being, participates in being, and is logically subordinate to being. (1:163)

The subordination of reason to being is a consequence of the notion of knowledge as participation. If reason is logically subordinate to being, it is impossible to imagine something that is not. If a symbol gains symbolic value by participating in that to which it points, it is impossible for reason or the imagination to create symbols that do not participate in being. There is no possibility of distance between the imagination or reason and that which is. This is the foundation of the ontological question.

The ontological question arises from the shock of nonbeing.

> The ontological question, the question of being-itself, arises in something like a "metaphysical shock"—the shock of possible non-being. (1:163)

The word *shock* here performs a function similar to that performed by the word *ecstasy* which Tillich employs elsewhere. Being-itself is beyond language and thus such an experience as that suggested by the "shock of non-being" could never be couched in language or thought. The "question" must be raised in a nonlinguistic form, just as it can only be "answered" in a nonlinguistic form through symbol and revelation. "Question" and "answer" are metaphorical. "Shock" and "ecstasy" are literally out of this world. Language serves as a catalyst, but the shock of nonbeing is a nonlinguistic experience. It is the experience that raises the question of being or God.

The question of being is beyond language. It is the question of the conditions of existence. But within the conditons of existence it is possible to construct categories and to do ontology.

> Ontology is possible because there are concepts which are less universal than being but more universal than any ontic concept, that is, more universal than any concept designating a realm of beings. Such concepts have been called "principles" or "categories" or "ultimate notions." (1:164)

The subject-object structure of reason, and the self-world structure of being that it presupposes, are not characteristic of being-itself. But within the conditions of existence this structure cannot be overcome. The analysis of this structure is the first step in any ontological analysis.

Ontological concepts are a priori. A priori concepts are those concepts which are omnipresent, encountered in every experience because they are the conditions of that experience.

> Those concepts are a priori which are presupposed in every actual experience, since they consitute they very structure of experience itself. The conditions of experience are a priori. (1:166)

A focus on the conditions of experience leads to the articulation of ontological concepts in impersonal structural terms. Transcendence is approached through the transcendentals.

There are four levels of ontological concepts:

> (1) the basic ontological structure which is the implicit condition of the ontological question; (2) the elements which constitute the ontological structure; (3) the characteristics of being which are the conditions of existence; and (4) the categories of being and knowing. (1:164)

The first level of the basic ontological structure (1) is the polarity between self and world and the subject-object structure of reason. Three pairs of elements constitute the second level of the structure (2). These pairs are individualization and participation, dynamics and form, freedom and destiny.[11] Each is an expression of the polar tension between the individual and the whole.

> In these three polarities the first element expresses the self-relatedness of being, its power of being something for itself, while the second element expresses the belongingness of being, its character of being a part of the universe of being.[12]

This tension, however, operates only within the polar conditions of existence, polarities that are transcended by being-itself or God.

The third level of the structure (3) deals with the distinction between essential and existential being. Access to this distinction is had through an analysis of freedom in finitude. "Finite freedom is the turning point from being to existence" (1:165). Again Tillich says that being or God is not essence as opposed to existence, but lies beyond the distinction of essence and existence. The fourth level of the structure (4) involves the categories of being and knowing. The four main categories to be analyzed are time, space, causality, and substance. Truth and goodness are not considered as ontological categories by Tillich because they are necessarily related to a judging subject. Since he is searching for categories that are a priori, which will articulate the conditions of knowing and judging, they must not be categories that depend for their reference on the acts of knowing and judging.

Those are the levels of the ontological structure. The analysis of this structure of finite being raises the question of the ground of the finite, which is the question of God. ". . . it is the finitude of being which drives us to the question of God" (1:166). Finite existence in itself is inexplicable. There is no separation between awareness of finitude and awareness of its ground. Ontological analysis of finitude drives not only to the question of God but also to the awareness of God as the ground of finite being. Similarly Tillich says that the quest for the New Being in Jesus as the Christ presupposes that being. Again this is the foundation provided by the onotlogical argument and the monistic approach.

> The quest for the New Being presupposes the presence of the New Being, as the search for truth presupposes the presence of truth. (2:80)

The quest is grounded in the structure of being. Reason participates in being and is subordinate to it.

The self-world structure of being and the subject-object structure of reason that it implies cannot be reduced. *Self* and *world* are correlative terms. A self has a world and it is in a world. A self cannot be derived from a world, nor is it possible to ask whether or not a self exists. It is an original phenomenon. The term *self* is applicable to beings other than man in some contexts, but it is only man who is aware of himself as a self, who has a world, and who is in a world:

> Every being participates in the structure of being, but man alone is immediately aware of this structure. It belongs to the character of existence that man is estranged from nature, that he is unable to understand it in the way in which he can understand man. (1:168)

> The term "self" is more embracing than the term "ego." It includes the subconscious and the unconscious "basis" of the self-conscious ego as well as self-consciousness (*cogitatio* in the Cartesian sense). Therefore, selfhood or self-centeredness must be attributed in some measure to all living beings and, in terms of analogy, to all individual *Gestalten* even in the inorganic realm. One can speak of self-centeredness in atoms as well as in animals, wherever the reaction to a stimulus is dependent upon a structural whole. Man is a fully developed and completely centered self. He "possesses" himself in the form of self-consciousness. He has an ego-self. (1:169–70)

Tillich alludes to Fichte's subjective idealism and Hobbes's objective realism as examples of the two types of reductionism with which the self-world polarity is threatened (1:171). The problem for Descartes was how to account for the relation and coordination between the thinking self and the external world. Tillich claims that there is no need to account for their coordination because they are correlative concepts. The polar structure of existence is a structure of which men are immediately aware. A person does not intuit the "I think" of Descartes. He intuits "I think about something." Subject and object, self and world, are in polarity even in the immediate intuition.[13] Men are driven to the question of God upon raising the question of what precedes or grounds the duality of self and world.

The self-world polarity is the basis for the subject-object structure of reason. In their use of language men must speak as subjects who experience objects. When the theologian employs the word *God* as an object, however, it can take on misleading ontological implications. In the use of language concerning God it must be acknowledged that the attempt is being made to convey something that is beyond the subject-object structure. Theology must include in its talk about God the acknowledgment that it cannot make God an object.[14]

In order to avoid the objectification of God, Tillich interprets man's knowledge of God as a participation in God's knowledge of himself. The subject-object structure cannot be transcended by man, but only by God:

> If there is a knowledge of God, it is God who knows himself through man. (cf. I Cor. 13:12) (1:172)

The interpretation of man's knowledge of God as a participation in God's self-knowledge is a basic tenet of idealism. Being and knowing accrue to the finite individual through participation in divine being and knowing. In moments of shock or ecstasy men are afforded a glimpse of the divine ground that transcends the structure of subject and object. Such a glimpse is correlative with the experience of finitude. These moments are rare. Thinking and acting take place within the structure of finite existence. The question of God is raised with the question of what underlies this structure. That question can be answered only by revelation. In the revelatory moment some image or person or event becomes transparent to the ground in which men recognize their own rootedness.

After his sketch of the polarity of self and world, Tillich goes on to set out the polarities that constitute the elements of the ontological structure. These elements are the polarities of individualization and participation, dynamics and form, and freedom and destiny. The first of these is the most crucial for the present study.

Tillich interprets individualization in such a way that the term *individual* gains its meaning from the experience of autonomy of a human self, rather than from the issue of one and many. This use of the personal self as the paradigmatic instance of individualization is significant because it allows Tillich to affirm individualization without compromising the monistic position that underlies his ontology.

> Individualization is not a characteristic of a special sphere of beings; it is an ontological element and therefore a *quality* of everything. It is implied in and constitutive of every self, which means that at least in an analogous way it is implied in and constitutive of every being. The very term "individual" points to the interdependence of self-relatedness and individualization. (1:174–75)

By defining individualization as a quality, Tillich steers away from metaphysical pluralism. Individualization, he says, is a quality that is implied in and constitutive of every being. Thus each petal of a flower, as a romantic poet might say, has its own individuality. Each snowflake and grain of sand possesses some of that quality. One could say that each of my roles in different aspects of my social life possesses the quality of individuality, as indeed it does, and still maintain that these are manifestations of a higher unity. Spinoza might also affirm the quality of individualization but would not allow a plurality of substance. A definition in terms of quality allows Tillich to avoid the connotations of autonomy that are associated with individualization in ordinary usage. The term *individualization* qualifies the substantive *being*. Thus it does not refer to a number of different entities. It is a quality of being. The term *individualization* functions here as does *centeredness* in Tillich's description of the self. Both appeal to the image of a focus or a node in order to portray individualization within an undifferentiated monism.

The fullness of individualization in the form of person and the fullness of individualization in the form of communion are correlative.

> No individual exists without participation, and no personal being exists without communal being. (1:176)

Communion appears only among persons, and an individual can be a person only in communion. Again it is important to note the way in which Tillich chooses his terms. He speaks of communion rather than of community. While this is only a nuance and not a definition, it is consonant with his interpretation of the language of pluralism within a monistic context. *Communion* contains the word *union* and carries connotations of mystical union that transcends individuality. *Community,* on the other hand, connotes a group of individuals who are related to one another through various forms of interdependence. The most salient form of such interdependence is human language. Language is mentioned once by Tillich in his discussion of communion, but the emphasis falls upon the universals in language and upon man as microcosm of the whole rather than upon the interdependent and social character of language.

> The universals make man universal; language proves that he is microcosmos. Through the universals man participates in the remotest stars and the remotest past. (1:176)

It is significant that Tillich is able to discuss communion without speaking of the social character of man.

Tillich views the polarity of individualization and participation as providing a solution to the debate between nominalists and realists. His characteristic procedure calls for him to criticize nominalism for affirming the individual and ignoring participation and to criticize realism for affirming participation while ignoring individualization.

Tillich does apply these criticisms, but he does it in such a way as to criticize nominalism roundly and to affirm "mystical realism," which emphasizes participation (1:177–78). He warns against allowing individuality and personality to disappear in some reality beyond the empirical. But he chooses the term *mystical realism,* both components of which fall on the realistic side of the realist-nominalist debate.

In his exposition of the ontological structure, Tillich has followed the basic form of his analysis, which is to discuss each term of a polarity and to affirm that the terms are correlative and cannot be separated. While he has followed this procedure in form, the emphasis in each case falls on the side of the unity of the whole rather than on the individual. First, individualization is defined as qualitative rather than quantitative. Next, communion rather than community is emphasized as the counterpart to person. Finally, the nominalistic reduction is firmly rejected and mystical realism is affirmed. This section provides an illustration of the strong leaning of Tillich's thought toward the metaphysical implications entailed by his monistic commitment, even while he discusses the polar tensions between the one and the many. Participation is correlated with individualization. While the language recalls the problem of the one and the many, metaphysical pluralism is never directly confronted.

Tillich concludes his section on the ontological elements with a description of the polarities of dynamics and form and freedom and destiny. Dynamics is related to chaos, unformed matter, the night, the emptiness that precedes creation, and to mythological and metaphysical notions of unbridled power:

> Dynamics, therefore, cannot be thought as something that is; nor can it be thought as something that is not. It is the *me on,* the potentiality of being, which is nonbeing in contrast to things that have a form, and the power of being in contrast to pure nonbeing. This highly dialectical concept is not an invention of the philosophers. It underlies most mythologies and is indi-

cated in the chaos, the *tohu-va-bohu,* the night, the emptiness, which precedes creation. It appears in metaphysical speculations as *Urgrund* (Böhme), will (Schopenhauer), will to power (Nietzsche), the unconscious (Hartmann, Freud), *élan vital* (Bergson), strife (Scheler, Jung). (1:179)

Tillich goes on to speak of the necessity of maintaining a tension between dynamics and form, but his equation of dynamics and unformed chaos is a description that places the dynamic aspect of being at the bottom of the chain of being and that associates it with disorder and chaos. Again the basic motifs of Platonic and Neoplatonic metaphysics are revealed.

Tillich chooses the polarity of freedom and destiny and rejects the opposition of freedom and necessity. Men experience themselves as destined, but not as determined. He criticizes the language of voluntarism and argues for a conception of freedom that is appropriate to the whole man:

> Freedom is not the freedom of a function (the "will") but of man, that is, of that being who is not a thing but a complete self, and a rational person. (1:183)

By arguing that freedom is to be conceived as a quality of the whole man and avoiding the language of will and voluntarism, Tillich is able to treat freedom as characteristic of wholes and to reject the notion of conflict between parts of a whole. The whole precedes the parts and gives them their character. The organic metaphor has often been used to suggest a harmony or at least an absence of conflict between parts, which nevertheless represent a certain amount of autonomy and ability to initiate activity. Tillich's description of the human body as a whole that transcends its parts provides the organic analogy that serves as a microcosm for the full system:

> Ontologically the whole precedes the parts and gives them their character as parts of this special whole. It is possible to understand the determinacy of isolated parts in the light of the free-

dom of the whole—namely, as a partial disintegration of the whole—but the converse is not possible. (1:184)

The freedom of the whole provides an interpretation for the determinacy of the parts. This is in accord with the Augustinian contention that true freedom lies in obedience to the divine will. Freedom is discovered and attained in correlation with one's destiny. Such freedom is an orientation to or attunement with the ground of one's being. Tillich's idea of freedom does not lead to a positive view of conflict between autonomous individuals. There is no need for negotiation, the development of social contracts, or the creation of new structures to mediate between the autonomy and interests of individuals and the common interests of society. Rather, there is an implicit faith that the interests of the individuals, when these individuals rightly understand themselves to be parts of the whole, will coincide with the structure of being or God. The freedom and destiny of finite beings is to be interpreted only in the light of being-itself. In the eschatological ideal, the interests and concerns of finite beings are fully aligned with those of God or being. Since Tillich does not allow for the choices and interest of finite beings to affect the divine being, the interpretation of the freedom and destiny of finite beings from the perspective of the divine life leads to a sacrifice of the interests and choices of finite individuals in favor of the divine being. This issue will be considered further in the examination of Tillich's doctrine of eschatology and of his view of time.

Tillich interprets the fact of negative judgment and of the estrangement that is characteristic of the human stituation as a testimony to the ontological character of nonbeing. If truth is understood to stem only from participation in being, then error must be described as estrangement from that participation or as participation in nonbeing. Estrangement and separation are warrants for the invocation of nonbeing (1:187). Nonbeing is a mystery. The world is composed of a dialectical participation of nonbeing in being. The problem of nonbeing is the problem of finitude.

"Finitude in awareness is anxiety" (1:191). In his description of the anxiety of finitude, Tillich deals serially with the categories of the understanding and the ontological elements of individualization and participation, form and dynamics, and freedom and destiny. In each case, a basic threat to personal existence is mediated through one of these elements and that threat is interpreted as ontological anxiety due to the threat of nonbeing. Anxiety is the immediate experiential base. Tillich follows Kierkegaard, Freud, and others in differentiating anxiety from fear. Anxiety has no specific object, is diffuse, and is therefore termed ontological and characteristic of all of human existence. Fear is due to a specific object and can be dealt with in relation to that object. Anxiety is fear of threat to one's very being. This experience is interpreted as facing the threat of nonbeing (1:191).

The infant is afraid of losing its mother. Of what is it afraid? It is afraid of nothing, but the nothing has a positive character. It is threatening and produces anxiety that is particularly crippling because there is no object with which to deal. This differs from the situation of the grown child who is torn between loyalty to his mother and loyalty to his father, or who is struggling to forge his own autonomy over against familial authority. In a case of divided loyalties there are two centers of power and attraction. This is the analogy that is employed in dualistic metaphysical systems in which life is interpreted as a struggle between devotion to God and service of the devil, between good and evil. The case of the infant and its mother is more appropriate to Tillich's discussion of the dialectical relationship between being and nonbeing. "To be finite is to be insecure" (1:195). This is consonant with Tillich's identification of dynamics and change with chaos and evil. Being is beyond the differentiations of existence. The mother is the universe or the ground of being at a time that is prior to the differentiations that occur as the infant begins to perceive himself as an autonomous person. Finitude is insecurity, and the awareness of finitude manifests itself through anxiety. Men confront anxiety with courage in the face of the threat of nonbeing. The infant learns to be courageous and to trust in the face of the chaotic world with which it is confronted.

In the lectures published as *The Courage to Be*, Tillich presents a fuller description of anxiety as the fundamental experience of the conditions of finite existence.[15] With anxiety as the experience of finitude, Tillich correlates courage as the response of faith. By choosing courage to represent faith, and positing it not as one virtue alongside others, but as the most comprehensive virtue, Tillich rejects the classical notion that the intellect is the highest and most characteristic human faculty. Anxiety and courage are more fundamental to the experience of the human condition than are ignorance and wisdom.

The Courage to Be includes a more elaborate phenomenological description of anxiety than is to be found in the *Systematic Theology*, but the implications for the present study are the same. Finite existence is without integrity, is characterized by ontological alienation and estrangement, and is experienced as anxiety. We long to overcome this anxiety, and we constantly strive to transform it into fear, to attribute it to particular objects and concrete threats within human existence. But ultimately these attempts are in vain. The real source of anxiety is nonbeing, which can never be transformed into an object. The only authentic response to this ontological anxiety is the courage to be, to take nonbeing into one's own being and to have faith in the face of anxiety.

Tillich delineates three major types of anxiety: the anxiety of fate and death, the anxiety of emptiness and meaninglessness, and the anxiety of guilt and condemnation. In each of these pairs, the first terms represents a relative threat to one's being, the second term an absolute one. In each case, anxiety is the experience of the threat of nonbeing, of a being's existential awareness of its possible nonbeing. The three types of anxiety reflect ontological, epistemological, and moral concerns respectively.[16]

Tillich closes his section on "Being and the Question of God" with an interpretation of the traditional arguments for the existence of God. They do not actually function as arguments, but they serve to express the question of God that is implied in human finitude. The ontological argument "gives a description of the way in which potential infinity is present in actual finitude."[17] It expresses the question concerning what is beyond essence and existence. This is the ontological question, which can be answered only be revelation. The Augustinian analysis of mind and memory and the Kantian critique of practical reason also raise this question by pointing to the element of the unconditional in the experience and conditions of finitude. The ontological approach stresses the continuity between human experience and the ground that underlies that experience.

The cosmological method, embracing the arguments traditionally referred to as cosmological and teleological, raises the question of the power of being in the face of the threat of nonbeing:

> In both cases [cosmological and teleological forms] the cosmological question comes out of the element of nonbeing in beings and meanings. No question of God would arise if there were no logical and noological (relating to meaning) threat of nonbeing, for then being would be safe; religiously speaking, God would be present in it. (1:209)

It is a question arising not out of the continuity of human existence and of the elements of potential infinity in the finite, but out of the experience of the dialectic of being and nonbeing in the finite situation. It arises out of the experience of threat. It is the question of the possibility of courage in the face of anxiety, of the power of being in the face of nonbeing (1:209).

THE CENTERED SELF

The chief concept employed by Tillich for discussing the unity of the self is that of *centeredness*. A personal self is centered. All beings are centered, but man is the only fully centered being (2:49). Tillich differentiates the "personal self" of human experience from the "psychological self," which is shared by animals (3:37). Animate and inanimate beings are centered to some extent, and animals can be the subject of psychological study, but they do not possess the fully developed ego of man. Tillich holds that the structures of existence can be probed only through the personal, because the one who is asking the questions is a human subject. The structures that are delineated in this manner, however, are applicable to nonhuman reality as well. Centeredness, like individualization and participation, is a quality of all being, but man is the only fully centered being.

There are several passages in the *Systematic Theology* where Tillich writes of the centeredness of the self.[18] The most extended treatment of the centered self is in the third volume. Centeredness is discussed as a universal phenomenon. Tillich's elucidation of the term creates a picture similar to Spinoza's portrayal of individuals as nodes in a field of forces, or as centers of action and passion within the single substance. *Centeredness* is a way of portraying individualization within a monistic framework. To describe a self or an object as centered is to describe it as focused, and is to remove attention from the question of external boundaries. It is a way of describing individuals without asserting distance between them. An entity is individuated by its center and not by its boundaries.

> The term "centeredness" is derived from the geometric circle and metaphorically applied to the structure of a being in which an effect exercised on one part has consequence for all other parts, directly or indirectly. . . . In this sense, centeredness exists under the control of all dimensions of being, but as a process of outgoing and returning. (3:33)

Tillich also speaks of a personal centeredness that is constituted by the moral dimension.

> Morality is the function of life in which the centered self constitutes itself as a person; it is the totality of those acts in which a potentially personal life process becomes an actual person. Such acts happen continually in a personal life; the constitution of the person as a person never comes to an end during this whole life process. (3:38)

> "Total centeredness" is the situation of having, face to face with one's self, a world to which one, at the same time, belongs as a part. (3:38)

This moral dimension includes interpersonal encounters. Within the polarities of the existential situation, men stand over against aspects of the being in which they participate. The realm of morality is that of the conditions of existence. Essential being is beyond morality. It is possible to speak of an ego-thou relation between God and man, but this language involves the use of an inadequate symbol. The monistic metaphysics embraces what might appear to be a dualistic relation.

> If we speak, as we must, of the ego-thou relation between God and man, the thou embraces the ego and consequently the entire relation. If it were otherwise, if the ego-thou relation with God was proper rather than symbolic, the ego could withdraw from the divine thou, because it includes the ego and is nearer to the ego than the ego to itself. (1:271)

Tillich's discussion of the centered self, then, does not threaten his monistic framework. Centeredness is a way of characterizing individualization within the ontology of the monistic type.

Sin as estrangement occurs when man's centeredness loses its orientation toward the divine center. Man is capable of attempting to make himself the center of his universe. This has been discussed above under the general notion of idolatry. When man attempts to elevate his own being into

an ultimate concern or center, this is a specific instance of
the general case of the elevation of anything finite into an
ultimate concern. Such an attempt to elevate one's own existence to the center of the universe is *hubris*.

> *Hubris* is not one form of sin beside others. It is sin in its total
> form, namely, the other side of unbelief or man's turning away
> from the divine center to which he belongs. It is turning toward
> one's self as the center of one's self and one's world. (2:50)

Because the conditions of existence inherently involve estrangement, *hubris* is always present in man's self-
affirmation. There is something about the affirmation of
one's own individuality that is sinful, just as finitude is inherently estranged and tragic.

> The quality of all acts in which man affirms himself existentially
> has two sides, the one in which he removes his center from the
> divine center (unbelief) and the other in which he makes him-
> self the center of himself and of his world (*hubris*). (2:51)

The affirmation of the individual self always involves a
component of *hubris* and estrangement. This is an aspect of
the tragic character of finitude. Distance of any kind involves
this tragic element. Tillich asserts the coincidence of creation and fall in a mysterious point. (1:255). The estrangement that characterizes existence is not due to sin alone, but
to the fact of finitude. Tillich makes this clear in mythological terms when he speaks of the command not to eat of the
fruit of the tree in Genesis 3 as indicative of a distance or
cleavage that already existed between man and God. This
distance existed before the mythological origin of the Fall in
man's act of disobedience.

> The divine prohibition presupposes a kind of split between
> creator and creature, a split which makes a command neces-
> sary even if it is given only in order to test the obedience of the
> creature. This cleavage is the most important point in the in-
> terpretation of the Fall. (2:35)

Even the initial appearance of individualization or centeredness constitutes a cleavage between man and God. In
estrangement, man is outside the divine center and he seeks
to return to it.

In an early article entitled "The Idea and the Ideal of
Personality" (1929), Tillich contrasts two alternative ways of
viewing the unity of the self in its relation to being of which
it is a part. The first is one in which the emphasis falls upon
opening oneself up to unity with all of the powers of being.
The unity of the self would be expanded to comprehend
the whole. The second alternative emphasizes the unity of
the self as an individual entity with emphasis upon discipline, autonomy, and self-control. The article stresses the
need for more attention to the first, to the openness of the
self to the fullness of being, and less stress on the ideal of
autonomy and self-control:

> It is presupposed that personality is that being which has power
> over its own being. This leaves two possibilities for any personal
> life. Either the *power* of being or the power *over* being prevails.
> In the first case, freedom, autonomy, and self-control are
> weakened or lost and pre-personal elements try to conquer the
> personal center; but at the same time, abundance of life, vital-
> ity, connection with all powers of being, and dynamic move-
> ment increase. Nothing is finished, nothing is subjected to a
> strict form, life is kept open. In the second case the fullness of
> life, its natural strength, is weakened or completely repressed;
> but, at the same time, concentration, self-control, discipline,
> stability, and consistency are created. Few creative possibilities
> remain, no "chaos" is left, life has ceased to be open. Since the
> second type has been promoted as the "ideal of personality," we
> can say that the conquest of the contemporary *ideal* of personal-
> ity in the name of the eternal *idea* of personality is the aim of the
> following analyses.[19]

When men try to create their own centers of autonomy,
instead of opening themselves to their proper centeredness
in the divine life they cut off the power of being that is able
to sustain growth and to provide new possibilities. Such an

attempt to build the autonomous personality is doomed to failure. Full centeredness is achieved by orientation toward the divine centeredness. Freedom and fulfillment of individuality occurs with the orientation of finite being toward its ground in the power of being.

PARTICIPATION AND THE RELIGIOUS SYMBOL

Within the monistic framework, knowledge is interpreted primarily as participation. In an article entitled "Participation and Knowledge: Problems of an Ontology of Cognition," Tillich treats the tension between separation and participation in the cognitive act much as he has treated the two types of philosophy of religion in his earlier article. He sketches the manner in which both participation and separation are involved in every cognitive act, and then moves to affirm the predominance of participation over separation. The tension between participation and separation is likened to that between existential knowledge and controlling knowledge and to that between metaphysical knowledge and scientific knowledge. As these analogies are constructed it becomes clear that Tillich sees participation as more fundamental and basic to knowing than is the moment of separation, even though some such moment is present in every act of knowing.

Tillich invokes three uses of the word *participation* in order to unpack the variety of meanings it contains. They are (1) "sharing," as in having shares in an enterprise, (2) "having in common," in the Platonic sense of *methexis* of the individual in the universal, or (3) "becoming a part," as of a political movement.[20] While the first and third of these definitions involve social participation, Tillich lifts out the element of identity as common to all three forms of participation.

> In all three cases participation points to an element of identity
> in that which is different or of a togetherness of that which is
> separated.[21]

The element of identity is correlated with the separation
implied in self-relatedness. Both identity and difference
are involved in the moment of knowing. Tillich's concern at
the outset of his article, however, is to show that participation is present even in the encounters that appear to involve
the most radical separateness, that of the invididual ego in
relation to other selves. Identity and difference are both
present, but the focus is already on the pole of identity.

The moment of encounter in knowing is a moment of
polarity or of opposition. But even this moment has connotations of meeting and thus participating in a common situation. In order for the cognitive encounter to occur, subject
and object must be open to receive each other. The presupposition of openness is "the potentiality of taking something
into one's own totality or of being taken into some other's
totality."[22] Such an encounter is also dependent upon the
moment of separation and detachment. Both moments are
present in any act of cognition. The moment of separation
and detachment is appropriate to scientific knowing, while
the moment of participation is appropriate to metaphysical
knowing (p. 203). Tillich then enters a short discussion of
phenomenological method in which he states that the element of participation, the structure of the presuppositions
of the knower in relation to the known, is more fundamental to the cognitive act than is the moment of separation.

> There is an irreducible though definite minimum of structural
> presuppositions of every cognitive encounter which are a
> genuine subject matter of phenomenological research. The
> evidence of their presence is apparent in the necessity of apply-
> ing them even in the act attacking their validity. I believe that
> the logical, categorical, and ontological principle, in short,
> everything which constitutes the structure of a cognitive
> encounter or, as previously formulated, the structure of asking
> questions, belong [sic] to this kind of being.

In this respect, participation seems to be absolutely predominant over separation. The subject is part of the process in which it not only encounters the object, but also encounters its own encountering. (P. 204; emphasis added)

The predominance is reinforced by Tillich's identification of the moment of participation with existential or saving knowledge, and the moment of separation with controlling knowledge. While this is offered as a description, it also serves an evaluative or persuasive function. The contrast between *existential or saving* and *controlling* is not neutral in the context of Tillich's own work. The former is much more fundamental and authentic. Apart from the normative connotations of the terms, however, Tillich is explicit in his contention that participation is the moment that is appropriate to metaphysical knowledge, and it is that knowledge with which we are primarily concerned.

Tillich goes on to stress the element of participation even in scientific knowing, and to criticize the predominance of the principle of separation in modern theories of knowledge. Again his examples are strongly weighted toward the side of participation as the authentic moment in knowing, even where the examples purport to be descriptive.

The infant experiences friendliness or anger with a situation before he objectifies the participants in this encounter as the father and himself. Participation precedes objectivation. If the stage of objectivation is reached, the other person may become an object of controlling knowledge. He can be tested, calculated, and handled, be it by a test-psychologist in America or by a propagandist in a totalitarian country or by a diplomatic husband or wife in any country. He has become an object of controlling knowledge. The communion of existential understanding, of understanding by participation, has been broken. (P. 206)

Insight in depth psychology is identified by Tillich as a form of knowledge as participation. Interpretation demands participation in the spiritual process that is expressed in a text.

The Socratic notion that knowledge creates virtue refers to the fact that knowledge is not controlling knowledge but cognitive participation in that which is essentially human. Finally, knowledge that involves commitment is characterized by a definitive predominance of participation.

> Participation within cognitive commitment means being grasped on a level of one's own reality and of reality generally which is not determined by the subject-object structure of finitude, but which underlies this structure. Commitment in this dimension does not mean the surrender of oneself as subject to an object, even the highest object, as popular theism demands. It means rather the participation of the whole personality in that which transcends objectivity as well as subjectivity. (P. 209)

Tillich claims that the elements of participation and separation are united in religious knowledge by the temporal structure of being. They are united by alternation between the several moments of cognition.

> Participation still persists in the moment of cognitive separation; the cognitive encounter includes moments of predominant participation, which I have called the perceptive moments, as well as moments of predominant separation, which I have called the cognitive moments. They alternate and establish in their totality a cognitive encounter. This is the situation in all realms, and it is the structure which makes religious knowledge possible. (P. 209)

It is important to note that while Tillich invokes the temporal character of knowing as the context in which the moments of participation and separation are united, he invokes it not in a linear, developmental way, but as an arena in which these moments alternate. There is no judgment that results from the comparison of two moments and leads to a synthesis that is compared to another perception and then further interpreted. Such an analysis of knowing as interpretation is given by Royce and leads to the conception of reality as social, which is characteristic of the third type.

Time provides the "space" in which the moments of the cognitive act alternate. All of Tillich's examples, however, as well as the explicit statement quoted above, point to participation as more fundamental to the cognitive act than separation, and as particularly characteristic of the existential knowledge involved in religion and metaphysics.

Tillich's doctrine of the religious symbol is an elaboration of the view of knowledge as participation. Religious symbols not only point to, but also participate in, the reality to which they refer. There is no distance between a symbol and the reality that it symbolizes. Communication between persons involves the use of symbols as catalysts to aid in the approach to a shared awareness, a participation in the experience of another. One shares with another symbols that point beyond themselves to that in which they participate. These symbols do not serve as arguments. They are pointers intended to direct the gaze of the person to whom they are addressed in order that he or she might also be grasped by or might intuit that aspect of being which is the appropriate referent of the symbol.

Tillich's doctrine of the religious symbol constitutes his account of the way in which religious language functions. It is not the case that symbolization represents one of many ways in which religious language is employed. Rather, it is the paradigmatic instance of such language.

> Religious symbols need no justification if their meaning is understood. For their meaning is that they are the language of religion and the only way in which religion can express itself directly. Indirectly and reflectively religion can also express itself in theological, philosophical, and artistic terms. But its direct self-expression is the symbol and the united group of symbols which we call myths.[23]

A symbol is distinguished by its participation in the reality to which it points. The reality to which a religious symbol points, and in which it participates, is being-itself. A religious symbol is distinguished from other symbols not by its content but by its function. Since everything participates in the ground of being, all signs and objects are capable, in the proper context, of serving as symbols for God. Symbols are born and die. In one cultural context a particular symbol (e.g., a cross) may serve a revelatory function, while in another that symbol may be incapable of providing an awareness of the participation of the finite in the infinite.

It is important to note that religious language for Tillich does not function as a tool for communication among persons. Rather, it functions to provide occasions for the awareness of the unity of all being in which that symbol, as well as the person for whom it is a symbol, participates. Religious language is not viewed as a social institution, but as a collection of symbols, each of which functions independently. Notice that in the above quotation Tillich describes myths as "united groups of symbols." The narrative character of myth is only the vehicle for groups of symbols. If Tillich had considered the difference between narrative and iconic symbols, he would have been led to address the social and temporal character of language and interpretation. These are the issues that predominate in the development of the third type.

In one sense it can be said that all language is symbolic. But the theory of symbolic language, and particularly of the function of religious symbols, offered by Tillich is one in which the symbol is lifted out of normal linguistic activity, just as the moment of ecstasy is one in which a saint is lifted out of his normal existence. The word *spirit*, as a religious symbol, functions exactly as do a Russian icon, the façade of an Indian temple, and the spires of Chartres. While the doctrine of the religious symbol is the basis for Tillich's discussion of religious language, it is not formulated with particular attention to the ways in which language functions.

Symbolic language functions in a catalytic manner in order to direct attention toward and to aid in the apprehension of that experience in which the symbol participates. To apprehend a symbol is to participate in its reality. For that reason, a symbol is self-authenticating. No interpretation is needed or possible. No external criteria can be brought to bear on it. It is impossible to compare a symbol with the reality that it is intended to represent, because there is no access to that reality apart from the symbol.

> Genuine symbols are not interchangeable at all, and real symbols provide no objective knowledge, but yet a true awareness. Therefore, the religious consciousness does not doubt the possibility of a true awareness of God. The criterion of the truth of a symbol naturally cannot be the comparison of it with the reality to which it refers, just because this reality is absolutely beyond human comprehension. The truth of a symbol depends upon its inner necessity for the symbol-creating consciousness.[24]

Symbols can be compared with one another, but it is unclear what are to be the criteria for such a comparison. In his early writing on symbols, Tillich speaks of the birth and death of symbols and of their self-authenticating character, their adequacy to the religious experience they express. In this view there is no possibility of comparing one symbol with another that is outside of the experience itself. In a paper delivered in 1960, he adds two criteria for the truth of a religious symbol:

> The negative quality which determines the truth of a religious symbol is its self-negation and transparency to the referent for which it stands. The positive quality which determines the truth of a religious symbol is the value of the symbolic material used in it. . . . The positive criterion for the truth of a symbol (e.g. creation) is the degree in which it includes the valuation in an ultimate perspective of the individual persons.[25]

A symbol can be judged to be more veridical than another symbol if (1) it is more fully transparent to that which it symbolizes, and (2) it places higher value on individual personality. The first criterion is independent of the content of a particular symbol. The demonic as well as the divine can be represented by a transparent symbol or event. The second criterion has been added later and is not further developed in Tillich's thought. The suggestion that symbols might be graded according to their ability to represent the personal as an ultimate value is something that Tillich avoided in his discussion of the adequacy of various symbols for God. It can be seen, however, as a more precise specification of the demand that symbols be adequate for the expression of a personal or existential experience. Thus a Gothic cathedral or Picasso's *Guernica* may be symbolic because they participate in and express the spirit of an individual, of a culture, and of the essentially human and personal.

Symbols provide no objective knowledge. Rather, they provide awareness. *Awareness* is a term that is appropriate to intuition or participation. It describes an apprehension or insight but is not something that can be brought within the subject-object situation and scrutinized. It cannot be made public in language. Language may serve as a catalyst for awareness, but the catalyst becomes totally transparent to that which is being symbolized or revealed. The ideal symbol or revelatory medium is one that becomes totally transparent to its referent. This is the case with Jesus of Nazareth as the Christ, who is the final revelation. His individuality is expanded and universalized to the point at which it becomes a revelation of being.

> Jesus of Nazareth is the medium of the final revelation because he sacrifices himself completely to Jesus as the Christ.[26]

A similar motif is expressed in the experience of the Christian. The saint is the one who most approximates transparency and who, in the moment of ecstasy, "stands outside of himself." The individual entity, whether symbol or person, reaches its fulfillment in the moment of its self-effacement and transparency to the whole.

> Revelation can occur through every personality which is transparent for the ground of being. . . . Saints are persons who are

transparent for the ground of being which is revealed through them and who are able to enter a revelatory constellation as mediums. (1:121)

Distance, comparison, and judgment are not involved in the revelatory moment. Revelation can have no criteria outside of itself. It must be self-authenticating. There is no way in which it can be subjected to rational scrutiny. Its truth is known by participation in that which it reveals.

By analogy, one must say that participation, not historical argument, guarantees the reality of the event upon which Christianity is based. It guarantees a personal life in which the New Being has conquered the old being. (2:114)

Tillich even goes so far as to say that the function and the truth of the religious symbol have nothing to do with the truth of the empirical assertions involved in it. Either an accurate or an inaccurate account of some part of human experience can serve with equal appropriateness as a symbol of ultimate reality.

The truth of a religious symbol has nothing to do with the truth of the empirical assertions involved in it, be they physical, psychological, or historical. A religious symbol possesses some truth if it adequately expresses the correlation of revelation in which some person stands. A religious symbol *is* true if it adequately expresses the correlation of some person with final revelation (1:240)

It should be noted that Tillich speaks of the criteria of truth here with the use of the verb *to express*. At this point Tillich has not only distinguished but completely separated the truth of the symbol as symbol from the truth of any empirical assertions that it might involve.

Immediacy in the relation between subject and object is inherent in the monistic type and appears in a different form in the individualistic type. Epistemological and ethical encounters in this first type have no distancing element. To

know the good is to do the good. Knowing involves participation, which involves being, which involves doing. It is
impossible to know that something is right and yet to choose
another course of action. From this perspective the ethical
man is one who immerses himself in the situation, who
participates to the fullest in the position in which he finds
himself. He does not and cannot turn outside the situation
to principles, criteria, or comparison with other experiences. Any such course would be an escape from the immediacy of the situation. Immediacy leads to contextualism
in ethics. Morality must be forged within the context of the
present without comparison of memories of the past or
anticipations of the future. This language is familiar from
the writings of the existentialists and from recent advocates
of "living life fully in the present."

Another consequence of the immediacy that is characteristic of this type is the impossibility of two persons coming to understand one another fully and continuing to disagree. Some would hold that it is possible for a theist to
define his terms, clarify the structure of his belief, make this
structure clear to another person, and the two could differ
over the truth of that belief.[27] The theist and the atheist
could disagree in the evaluation of common data or on the
basis of confirming experience on the part of one and not
on the part of the other. But Tillich would not accept this
description of the situation. It is not possible to know God
or being-itself without perceiving one's own participation in
this being. Thus it is impossible to come to a cognitive understanding of theistic belief, and then to set out to decide
whether or not such a belief is true. This would be to attempt to place God within the subject-object categories that
are employed in judgments concerning objects. Such a conception would bear no relation to the God who is beyond
the gods. Symbols cannot be compared with that to which
they refer because it is beyond human comprehension, except through the symbolic consciousness.

Tillich refers to the "Thomistic dissolution" of the Augustinian solution.[28] He means that once immediacy has been lost, once the mystical union has been dissolved and attention is focused on the differences and distances between persons and objects, the original unity cannot easily be recovered. This dissolution, he says,

> has, for the larger part of Western humanity, undermined the ontological approach and with it the immediate religious certainty. It has replaced the first type of phiolsophy of religion with the second type. (P. 16)

Tillich claims that the move from the first to the second type involves the move from immediate rational certainty to submission to external authority.

> The general character of the Thomistic approach to the philosophy of religion is the following: the rational way to God is not immediate, but mediated. It is a way of inference which, although correct, does not give unconditional certainty; therefore it must be completed by the way of authority. This means that the immediate rationality of the Franciscans is replaced by an argumentative rationality, and that beside this rational element stands non-rational authority. (P. 16)

The use of the word *authority* here in juxtaposition with Thomas invokes the image of the authority structure of the Roman Church and the heteronomy that that involves. It is true that this is related to the Thomistic move. But it is possible to subject intuition to scrutiny through public comparison and judgment without submission to a heteronomous authority. Tillich's illustration serves to equate mediation with such submission. This is misleading.

    The ideal extrapolation of the monistic type is the mystical experience of oneness with the whole or the experience of the infant prior to and during its initial differentiation from the mother. It is prior to the realization of autonomy and the raising of the issue of rebellion in the face of authority. The relation of the infant to its mother, of the mystic to the infinite, is a trusting, or a merger of the self with the larger whole. Tillich is correct when he says that for the larger part of Western humanity the ontological approach has been undermined, and with it immediate religious certainty. This is the realization of the child or the adult that the world of safety in the bosom of his mother cannot be regained. It is gone forever, and with it the certainty that was provided by that world.

The question of external authority arises only with the admission that the world includes a plurality of persons and powers, and that some of these are external to others. This is to admit real distance. Once this externality is taken as the focus, immediate knowledge of the absolute or infinite is destroyed. Certainty is no longer guaranteed. Judgments must be made. Faith is not only a stance. It is not a matter of standing in a particular spot and having a certain perspective or apprehension. Judgments in theological matters must be weighed and examined and acted upon in a way analogous to all other judgments. Intuition and immediate certainty are not attainable.

TIME AND ESCHATOLOGY

In the third volume of the *Systematic Theology*, published in 1963, Tillich completed his system with sections on "Life and the Spirit" and "History and the Kingdom of God." In both of these sections and in the introduction to the final volume he expressed indebtness to the recent interest in philosophy of life with its orientation toward process and growth.[29] Attention to the ambiguities of life and history requires that in this volume he give some prominence to time, change, and movement in his phenomenology of human existence. By focusing on his treatment of eschatology it will be possible to observe his portrayal of the relation between finite and infinite as he conceives its fulfillment.

Discussions of the state of nature in Eden and of the end of history or the kingdom of God may appear to strain the credulity of contemporary readers. As mythical expressions, however, such speculation can be revealing. It often exposes the images in terms of which a thinker conceives the ideal relationship between man and his fellows or man and God. A portrayal of the adamic state of natural man or a description of the conditions of life in the kingdom of God may reveal an author's projection of the ideal or essential conditions of life, abstracted from the complexities of mundane existence.[30]

Similarly discussions of the beginning and end of time reveal the way in which an author conceives of the nature of time. The different interpretations of time in each of the three types under consideration are significant for a differentiation of the types. The monistic type, as represented by Tillich, yields a metaphysical system that is basically atemporal. This characteristic is closely related to the problem of mediacy and immediacy in knowing and thus to the theories of language that issue from each of the types. If language is understood to have a social character that mediates knowledge and communication, it is necessary to recognize the fact that speaking and listening occur in time. The moment of shock or ecstasy that might be occasioned by a particular revelatory symbol, however, is conceived as a moment that does not endure. It may occur in time, but it does not take time. It is an atemporal conception similar to that of the "knife-edge present" to which William James referred.

It will be demonstrated in the following chapter that the individualistic type yields a metaphysics that is also atemporal. The immediate encounter between ego and other is also conceived as a fleeting moment that reveals, but does not endure. Thinkers who represent both monistic and individualistic types subscribe to the notion that the goal of knowing is an immediate relationship between knower and known. If immediacy is the goal, then knowing is successful only when it manages to escape time.

In Tillich's thought time and history provide the occasion

for the participation of beings in the ground and power of their being, which has its real signifiance as an atemporal, eternal condition. Space and time are categories of finitude, as are causality and substance. They are comprehended within the larger structure of being, the self-world polarity, and the ontological elements. The self-world structure and the elements are atemporal in the sense that they transcend time and space. This treatment of time continues even when Tillich is dealing explicitly with history and the processes of growth.

The most significant term in Tillich's discussion of eschatology is the term *essentialization*. The end of history is the essentialization of all things. Tillich admits that this is a "somewhat Platonizing answer" and attributes the term to Schelling.[31] The concept of essentialization is consonant with his basic scheme of the relation between finite and infinite. Man is finite freedom involved in the polarities and the estrangement of existence. The end of history is a movement beyond this existential state with its tensions and a reunion of man with the essential being of God. The drama of history is composed of the move from man's essential union with God to the existential conditions of history that are the consequences of the fall, and back to the essential union of salvation. This drama is enacted both in the life of each individual and in history as a whole.

> The theological problem of eschatology is not constituted by the many things which will happen but by the one "thing" which is not a thing but which is the symbolic expression of the relation of the temporal to the eternal. More specifically, it symbolizes the "transition" from the temporal to the eternal, and this is a metaphor similar to that of the transition from the eternal to the temporal in the doctrine of creation, from essence to existence in the doctrine of the fall, and from existence to essence in the doctrine of salvation. (3:395)

Does this move from the essential to the existential and back to the essential, from creation through fall to salvation, add to the totality of being? Does history mean anything for God? Is the kingdom of God any improvement over creation? These issues are raised not only by philosophies of process and growth but also by earlier theological discussions of the process of salvation and of the relationship between justification and salvation. Process theologians of various sorts have held that history is the arena of God's becoming and that God gains in being and value through the actual movement of history.[32] In contrast, the Platonic tradition in which Tillich stands has held that God is uninfluenced by history. Being-itself is unchanging. History is regarded as an occasion in which those aspects of being which are estranged or alienated from their ground seek to return.

The emphasis upon trust, on estrangement from the home in which one has found comfort and rest and from the ground of one's being, leads to a notion of being that is unchanging, steady, and omnipresent. The infant wishes to be reunited with the bosom of the mother. It does not want to join with the mother in the accomplishment of some task. Neither the infant nor the mystic is seeking a friend, a colleague, or a partner. Rather, they want a bosom, a home, a basis for trust. A process metaphysics such as that of Hartshorne[33] emphasizes the cooperation of man with God in bringing about his kingdom. This is not an equal cooperation. It is still an asymmetric relation but is more analogous to the partnership between father and son than to that between mother and infant, which is centered on trust, on the anxiety of estrangement, and on the eros toward reunion with that from which one is estranged.

The *telos* of history is eternal life.

> The end of history in the sense of the inner aim or the *telos* of history is "eternal life."[34]

Eternity triumphs over time, not only at the close of history but also as the *telos* of each moment. Past and future meet in the present, which is the eternal now. History and the temporal provide the arena in which the eternal is encountered. It is that eternal element which is essential both now and at the end of history. Men stand now in the face of the eternal looking toward the end of history.

> In accord with the predominance of the present in temporal experience, eternity must first be symbolized as an eternal present (*nunc eternum*). But this *nunc eternum* is not simultaneity or the negation of an independent meaning of past and future. The eternal present is moving from past to future, but without ceasing to be present. (1:275)

The present is predominant. Immediate experience is the ideal. Past and future require memory and anticipation. Neither can be immediate. It is the present that offers immediacy.

An indication of the Platonic and monistic vision that informs Tillich's metaphysics can be seen in his treatment of the demonic at the end of history. The negative is eliminated from eternal life. It is not remembered. It never existed. An ambivalence appears in the attempt to state that the negative has some influence in that it is overcome by the positive, which is elevated into eternal life. The eternal involves a transcending of that which is negative and tragic and which belongs to the existential conditions of estrangement.

The appearance of evil vanishes in the face of the eternal (3:399).

> If we apply again the metaphor of "eternal memory," we can say that the negative is not an object of eternal memory in the sense of living retention. Neither is it forgotten, for forgetting presupposes at least a moment of remembering. The negative is not remembered at all. It is acknowledged for what it is, nonbeing. Nevertheless it is without effect on that which is eternally remembered. It is present in the eternal memory as that which is conquered and thrown out into its naked nothingness (for example, a lie). (3:400)

This is Tillich's interpretation of the last judgment and of the separation of good from evil. It also serves a Platonizing function of expunging any trace of conflict, evil, and struggle from essential being and its final fulfillment. The negative is not forgotten because that would mean that it had once had some status and that some attention was directed toward it. It is conquered and yet it never really was.

In the development of his notion of essentialization Tillich states that what history adds to essential being is this conquest of the negative in time.

> But the term "essentialization" can also mean that the new which has been actualized in time and space adds something to essential being, uniting it with the positive which is created within existence, thus producing the ultimately new, the "New Being," not fragmentarily as in temporal life, but wholly as a contribution to the Kingdom of God in its fulfillment. . . . Participation in the eternal life depends upon a creative synthesis of a being's essential nature with what it has made of it in its temporal existence. In so far as the negative has maintained possession of it, in so far as the essential has conquered existential distortion its standing is higher in eternal life. (3:400–401)

Tillich builds temporal experience into his notion of New Being, but he retains the image of exile and return, of going out and returning to essential being. Morality, culture, and religion come to an end at the end of history. Each of these presupposes a distance that is a consequence of the polarities of existence and that has no place in eternal life.

Tillich interprets fulfillment of life or salvation as the elevation of man to union with God in the ground of being, but he has also portrayed created existence as estrangement from this ground with which man was once united. His is a doctrine of redemption as restoration. The restoration is union with God. Essentialization is the reunion of finite, existential being with the essential ground of its existence, now renewed by expunging the negative. The process of renewal is not portrayed in the language of growth or transformation. Rather, it is portrayed as the elimination of the negative.

At several points Tillich speaks directly of the relation between time and the eternal in the fulfillment. His language suggests that some aspect of the temporal remains in the eternal in order to give living character to eternal life. But the temporal is absorbed into the eternal in the spirit of the eternal return and of monistic union.

> The transition from the temporal to the eternal, the "end" of the temporal, is not a temporal event——just as the creation is not a temporal event. Time is the form of the created finite (thus being created with it), and eternity is the inner aim, the *telos* of the created finite, permanently elevating the finite into itself. With a bold metaphor one could say that the temporal, in a continuous process, becomes "eternal memory." But *eternal* memory is living retention of the remembered thing. It is together past, present and future in a transcendent unity of the three modes of time. (3:399)

Participation in eternity is "the creative act of God, who lets the temporal separate itself from and return to the eternal" (3:410). God is unchanging. Philosophies of becoming or process "contradict too obviously the fundamental theological doctrine of God's impassability" (3:404).

The eternal, unchanging character of God results from an emphasis upon security and the elimination of contingency. In his essay "Two Types of Philosophy of Religion," Tillich reiterates several times the difference between the ontological and the cosmological method as the issue of certainty of faith versus the contingent in religion. The cosmological method, which allows for a plurality of entities in the universe, does not provide the certainty, the assurance, and the trust that is possible within the embracing, maternal character of the ontological method. Thus it is important to Tillich to maintain the essence, the eternity, the unchanging character of God.

Time and change are present in the divine life, but they are contained there within an eternal unity. Time and change have been lifted out of time. In reference to the contrast between the Greek notion of time as cyclical and the Augustinian portrayal of history as linear, Tillich suggests a kind of curve of the eternal return.

> I would suggest a curve which comes from above, moves down as well as ahead, reaches the deepest point which is the *nunc existentiale*, the "existential now," and returns in an analogous way to that from which it came, going ahead as well as going up. This curve can be drawn in every moment of experienced time, and it can also be seen as the diagram for temporality as a whole. It implies the creation of the temporal, the beginning of time, and the return of the temporal to the eternal, the end of time. (3:420)

There is a constant movement from the essential and eternal out into the existential and temporal and then back into the essential and eternal. This movement itself is not in time, but is an eternal movement. Time is the occasion for this movement but the temporal is not essential to the relation between finite and infinite.

The relations of the existential and the essential and of the temporal and the eternal in the fulfillment have been discussed. A third significant relation is that between individualization and participation in eternal life. The interpretation of this chapter would suggest that individuality is not preserved in the fulfillment and that individuals are taken up and absorbed into the infinite. This is the implication of Tillich's monistic commitments. Tillich appears to qualify those commitments to the extent of speaking of a new preservation of centered selves, now centered in the divine life. Divine centeredness, creativity, and freedom or destiny (there is no difference between freedom and destiny in the essential state) have replaced centeredness, creativity, and the freedom and destiny of individual selves. True individuality in the state of blessedness is full surrender and participation in the divine life.

To use another terminology, we can say that in Eternal Life the

8484 GOD AND THE SELF

center and through it is in communion with all other personal
centers. Therefore the demand to acknowledge them as persons and to unite with them as estranged parts of the universal
unity is not needed. Eternal life is the end of morality because
what morality demanded is fulfilled in it. (3:402)

In the ideal state there is no distance between individuals.
There is no ethical distance. There can be no conflict and
there is no need for negotiation or interpretation because
there is no differentiation. It is impossible to separate freedom from destiny or the eternal destiny of any individual
from that of the race. The finite has returned to the infinite
and the process of essentialization is complete.

The rhythm from essence through existential estrangement to essentialization is one that draws all things back into
union with the whole. The centeredness of selves has given
way to the divine centeredness of being-itself. The historical
existence of selves in time has given way to the eternal
memory, a metaphor that refers again to the one substance,
to being-itself. Salvation is restoration. It is the reunion of
the infant with the mother, the return to oneness with the
whole. This is the *telos* of the mystical element in religious
experience and is one aspect of every doctrine of God. In
the monistic type it becomes the governing motif for the
interpretation of the nature of God and of the relation of
finite to infinite.

Tillich's monism finally eliminates all distinctions and
thus, as we have seen, cannot adequately describe the integrity of the individual or express the experience of autonomy. Tillich draws on and develops sophisticated
analyses of the existential conditions of human finitude, but
these are set within the context of a monism in which such
conditions are held to be penultimate. All relations, such as
those of space and time, are internal to the ground of being,
which is God. Tillich's phenomenological analyses of anxiety, faith, and the spirit are more sophisticated than his
metaphysical system might suggest. In his descriptions of

the existential conditions of human finitude, he is sensitive to the experience of autonomy and freedom. Systematically, however, he views autonomy as idolatry or sin, and places emphasis on the centering of the self within the system of being. Knowledge is defined as participation in the being of the object that is to be known. God as the ground of being transcends all personhood. The goal of human nature, the kingdom of God, is portrayed as essentialization, the overcoming of the estrangement that characterizes finite existence. There is no place in this system for an autonomous person or agent who is distinct from other person or agents.

The second type follows from this insufficiency in the monistic view. It is a conception of the universe that begins with the notion of the individual. Individuals form the fundamental constituents of reality. They are related to one another, but they exist as discrete individuals. Their relations are external relations that are not essential to their integrity as individuals. When such individuals are persons, their autonomy is stressed.

NOTES

1. Paul Tillich, "The Two Types of Philosophy of Religion," *Theology of Culture*, ed. R. Kimball (New York: Oxford University Press, 1959), pp. 10–11.

2. Paul Tillich, *Systematic Theology* (Chicago: University of Chicago Press, 1951), 1: 163–204.

3. Ibid. (1957), 2: 23.

4. James Luther Adams, *Paul Tillich's Philosophy of Culture, Science and Religion* (New York: Harper and Row, 1965), p. 37.

5. *Systematic Theology*, 1: 245.

6. Ibid. 1: 279.

7. This interpretation of knowledge as participation is also found in Karl Barth's *Church Dogmatics*. Barth's doctrine of the knowledge of God reveals the philosophical idealism that informs much of that work. Barth emphasizes the freedom of God to reveal himself. But this freedom demands that God take man's act of knowing up into his own act of knowing himself. In man's knowledge of God "this existence of ours is enclosed within the act of God." See Karl Barth, *Church Dogmatics*, ed. G. W. Bromiley and T. F. Torrance, trans. G. T. Thomson (Edinburgh: T. & T. Clark, 1936), 1/1: 529. Barth is anxious to disallow any human knowledge of God because he assumes that knowing is being, and thus for man to know God would be to compromise the infinite distance between man and God.

86   GOD AND THE SELF

8. *Systematic Theology*, 1: 206.
9. Paul Tillich, *Dynamics of Faith* (New York: Harper and Brothers, 1957), p. 22.
10. *Systematic Theology*, 2: 45.
11. In his list of the three pairs of elements that constitute the basic ontological structure, Tillich refers to the first pair as "individuality and universality" (*Systematic Theology*, 1: 165). When he begins to consider the specific elements, he refers to this first pair as "individualization and participation" (ibid., 1: 174ff.). This shift allows him to "Platonize" both poles of the original pair.
12. *Systematic Theology*, 1: 165.
13. The phenomenological analysis here is similar to that of Friedrich Schleiermacher in his discussion of the feeling of relative freedom over against the world and the feeling of relative dependence upon the world. See Friedrich Schleiermacher, *The Christian Faith*, trans. H. R. Mackintosh and J. S. Stewart (Edinburgh: T. & T. Clark, 1928), pp. 12–18.
14. *Systematic Theology*, 1: 172–73.
15. Paul Tillich, *The Courage to Be* (New Haven, Conn.: Yale University Press, 1952).
16. The three types of anxiety are similar to the three experiential challenges to the ability to make sense out of one's existence, as delineated by Geertz:
There are at least three points where chaos—a tumult of events which lack not just interpretations but *interpretability*—threatens to break in upon man: at the limits of his analytic capacities, at the limits of his powers of endurance, and at the limits of his moral insight. Bafflement, suffering, and a sense of intractable ethical paradox are all, if they become intense enough or are sustained long enough, radical challenges to the proposition that life is comprehensible and that we can, by taking thought, orient ourselves effectively within it—challenges with which any religion, however "primitive," which hopes to persist must attempt somehow to cope. (Clifford Geertz, *The Interpretation of Cultures* [New York: Basic Books, 1973], p. 100)
While both Tillich and Geertz consider the same three areas of experience, Geertz emphasizes the cognitive or interpretive component of chaos while Tillich emphasizes the affective component of anxiety and suggests that it must be dealt with on a level that is more fundamental than the cognitive.
17. *Systematic Theology*, 1: 206.
18. See *Systematic Theology*, 1: 184, 186; 2: 60–63; 3: 32–50, 234.
19. Paul Tillich, "The Idea and the Ideal of Personality," *The Protestant Era*, trans. J. L. Adams (Chicago: The University of Chicago Press, 1948), p. 119.
20. Paul Tillich, "Participation and Knowledge: Problems of an Ontology of Cognition," *Sociologica*. Aufsätze, Max Horkheimer zum sechzigsten Geburtstag gewidmet. Vol. 1: "Frankfurter Beiträge zur Soziologie," ed. T. W. Adorno and W. Dirks (Frankfurt am Main: Europäische Verlagsanstalt, 1955), p. 201.
21. *Ibid.*
22. Tillich, "Participation and Knowledge," p. 202.
23. Paul Tillich, "The Meaning and Justification of Religious Symbols," *Religious Experience and Truth: A Symposium*, ed. S. Hook (New York: New York University Press, 1961), p. 3.
24. Paul Tillich, "The Religious Symbol," *Religious Experience and Truth: A Symposium*, ed. S. Hook (New York: New York University Press, 1961), p. 316.
25. Tillich, "The Meaning and Justification of Religious Symbols," pp. 10–11.
26. *Systematic Theology*, 1: 136.
27. See John Wisdom's parable of the gardener quoted in "Theology and Falsification: The University Discussion" in *New Essays in Philosophical Theology*, ed. A. Flew and A. MacIntyre (London: SCM Press, 1955), p. 96.
28. "The Two Types of Philosophy of Religion," p. 16.

29. *Systematic Theology*, 3: 5.

30. Barth's *Church Dogmatics*, for example, includes long sections on the virgin birth and angelic life that are not naive statements, but are crucial to the theological position that Barth develops in that work. See idem, 1/2: 172–202, 3/3: 369–531.

31. *Systematic Theology*, 3: 400.

32. For examples, see Jonathan Edwards, "Dissertation on the End for Which God Created the World," *Works,* ed. S. E. Dwight (New York: G & C & H Carvill, 1830), 3: 3–89 and Charles Hartshorne, *The Divine Relativity* (New Haven, Conn.: Yale University Press, 1948).

33. Hartshorne, *The Divine Relativity*.

34. *Systematic Theology*, 3: 394.

3

The Self as Will or Agent: The Individualistic Type

The second typical conception is that of a pluralistic and individualistic metaphysics. The universe is composed of a number of individuals that are related to each other externally. Instead of all relations being internal to a single substance that is God or being-itself, relations obtain between individuals whose integrity is not dependent upon those relations. The individual is prior to the whole. While this second type may be illustrated by a materialistic metaphysics that attempts to reduce all entities to physical atoms, the individualistic type is represented as well by contemporary existentialist philosophy, in which autonomy is taken to be the fundamental characteristic of persons. Whether the atoms in question be physical units or autonomous selves, *atomism* is a term that refers to a conception of the world as an aggregate of indivisible individuals. The paradigmatic unit in the monistic type is the whole, and the part is defined in terms of the whole. The paradigmatic unit in this second type is the individual, and the whole is understood to be a group of individuals. The ultimate dissolution of individuals and plurality generally in Tillich's conception of the final essentialization of all things leads to an attempt to conceive of the world in individualistic terms.

This type will be illustrated by a brief consideration of the influence of existentialist thought in theology and by analysis of the work of Austin Farrer. In *Finite and Infinite* (1943) Farrer attempted to reconstruct the classical notion of finite substance in order to aid his readers in its apprehension. This reconstruction begins with an analysis of will and of the unity that is discovered in the act of willing. It is then expanded to a conception of the self, from which it is generalized to include other finite entities. The apprehension of substance, according to Farrer, must begin with the apprehension of the unity to which an individual has most direct access. That unity is the self considered as the subject of its acts. The unity of the autonomous self becomes the paradigm for a consideration of finite substance.

THE TYPE

Within schemes of the second type, being is not one but is many. The world is an aggregate of units, whether these units be physical atoms, extended things and thinking beings, monads, facts, or existential selves. Many substances are posited. This position does not emphasize the relation of part to whole, in which a part has integrity only as it participates in the whole. It is more akin to the model provided by kinetic theory for the activity of molecules in a closed container than it is to the notion of a plenum. There are many units, atoms, or substances that are distant from one another and that interact in various ways.

In the monistic vision, all boundaries, external relations, distances between persons, events, and even values are viewed as finally illusory. No distinction can be so fundamental as the unity that transcends it. Boundaries and discriminations of all sorts are conditions of finitude, of our limited knowledge, of an estrangement that is not ultimate and that may one day be overcome. In the individualistic vision, however, particular entities are defined by their

boundaries and by their differentiation from others. Boundaries and distances are basic to the identification of the
primitive units. The unity of the whole is not fundamental,
but is approached additively through a summation of individuals that make up the world. Being is not a simple or
primitive notion. It is an abstraction employed to refer to
the common ontological status of everything that is.

The difference in the two types with respect to discrimination is crucial. An individual is defined in terms of boundaries and criteria for discriminating it from what it is not. *A
is not not-a*. While the criteria for discriminating one physical atom from another or one person from another may be
difficult to specify, some such discrimination must in principle be possible. Atoms that are physically similar, for instance, may be distinguished by their positions in space and
time.

In contrast, the monistic type represents a conception in
which all such boundaries and criteria for discrimination
are finally unreal. All divisions conceal an underlying unity.
For Tillich that unity is the ground of all being in which all
beings participate and to which they long to return. In the
individualistic context, no such ground exists. The paradigm of unity is the unit, the individual entity.

It was appropriate to begin the sketch of the monistic
type with a consideration of ontology, and it is appropriate
to begin here with a consideration of epistemology. In the
monistic context, the identity of the self is conceivable only
as a part of the whole in which it participates. To see it in
relation to that whole, within the context of the basic ontological structure, is crucial. The self does not exist in isolation. The ontological question is prior. In the individualistic
type, the self is given as a primitive concept. The problem is
to discover one's own identity and to make contact with the
rest of the world. Solipsism is always a threat, and the epistemological issue is always fundamental. Issues such as the
"problem of the external world" and the "problem of other
minds" do not arise in the monistic context. They arise only

when one begins with the individual and sets out to examine the validity of his perceptions and judgments. Epistemology is the characteristic concern of the second type, as ontology is the characteristic concern of the first.

Epistemology. The knowledge that a self has of itself is primary and immediate. This is a private knowledge that is available to the self with an immediacy unavailable to anyone else. Knowledge of other selves and of things, even knowledge of God, is either secondary, mediated knowledge or is an encounter or apprehension to which one has been directed by the use of analogy. The behavior of others is observed and the self projects upon that behavior the pattern of unity and self-knowledge that it enjoys. By analogy, a self is attributed to the other. The recognition of analogous structures, rather than the participation of a symbol in the reality to which it points, is the primary mode of knowing.

The ontological argument is impossible, but the cosmological argument is quite appropriate. If knowing is not participation, it is impossible to move from a limited or parochial knowledge to the ground in which that limited knowledge participates. This is the movement of the ontological argument. It is possible, however, to move from knowledge of individuals to knowledge of their effects or causes. Individuals affect one another. Experiments may be designed, as in the case of an investigation of the laws of motion in physics, to follow a chain of causation backward or forward in time and to map the collisions and effects of individuals on each other. This is the basis for the cosmological argument.

Tillich affirms the ontological approach as fundamental to religious knowledge. Insofar as the cosmological argument contains a true insight, it is the ontological insight of participation, which may be embedded in a form of argument labeled cosmological. One of the differences between the monistic and individualistic types is manifested in the appropriateness of the ontological or cosmological approaches to knowledge of God. It is not surprising then to find Farrer affirming the cosmological and rejecting the ontological except to the extent that it might contain a hint of the insight embodied in the cosmological approach.

> For however many bases dialectic may appear to take, its principle must always be the cosmological idea which analysis is to analyse: the idea of God as effecting the world and the world as the effect of God. In this sense all the proofs can be reduced to the cosmological . . . The only exception seems to be the heretical argument of Anselm. It is not surprising to find this to be an exception since it is not an argument. It claims that we have a self-authenticating apprehension of God in and by Himself. Were this an appeal to a mystical Ineffable, it might convince those who are privileged to enjoy it; but as it attempts to prove its case from a description or definition of God which can be stated, it fails immediately because the description is in terms of the creation and manifestly defines God through a function which he exercises relatively thereto. To make the proof good we must scrutinize this function, and so we fall into an analysis of the cosmological idea after all.[1]

It should be noted that Anselm does not define God in reference to the creation. Anselm's formulation of the ontological argument is classic, and Farrer is trying to bring him within the scope of the cosmological approach. But Anselm takes his departure from a scrutiny of the meaning of his formula for God. It is Descartes who later presents a formulation of the ontological argument that invokes creation by asking for the cause of the idea of God in us. Descartes is the author of a pluralist metaphysic, and his meditations are cited by Farrer as a "pleasant and naive expression of the elements of theistic thinking," where *theistic* is here taken to imply pluralism in contrast to the pantheistic character of monism.[2] As Tillich subsumes the cosmological under the ontological approach, Farrer is attempting to subsume the ontological under the cosmological. Scrutiny of the function of creation involves us in the traditional consideration of proximate and ultimate causation, and thus in an analysis of the cosmological idea.

The point of origin for this mapping of a causal chain may be either the individual self apprehended as both cause and effect, or individual subjects or objects that inhabit the world. There is a tendency in the epistemological thought of this type for these starting points to diverge so that different kinds of knowing are ascribed to knowledge of persons and knowledge of things. This divergence has become a dichotomy in some existentialist quarters, particularly in Buber's distinction between "I-thou" and "I-it" relations.[3] The former term refers to encounters between persons as subjects in which a kind of romantic immediacy is discovered. The second refers to the perception of another as an object, whether that other be inanimate or another person conceived in third-person terms. These are held to be different forms of knowing with the strong implication that subject-subject encounters are superior to the perception of another as object. This dichotomy is another consequence of the insistence upon striving for immediacy in knowing. There is no recognition of the interplay between second- and third-person language in the perception of other individuals. There is little recognition even of the role of language in knowing.

Knowing according to this conception proceeds by the projection of analogies and the judgment as to their relevance or appropriateness. The role of the will in judging enters in a way that it does not enter the doctrine of symbols and of knowledge by participation. Both Farrer and the existentialists share this emphasis on man as will. Farrer does not accept the dichotomy between I-it and I-thou relations and he attempts to move from an analysis of will to a description of an embodied self and then to a more generalized substance formula. Although the existentialist influence has been the most prominent mode in which the emphasis upon man as individual will has been set, Farrer's work has been chosen for close analysis because he adopted the voluntaristic approach and used it to transform the traditional metaphysical portrayal of finite individuals and of the movement to apprehension of the infinite. While Farrer does not do philosophy in the dramatic or autobiographical form often characteristic of existentialism, the reconstruction of substance so that it is understood primarily as will is a systematic attempt to do philosophical theology on the basis of the voluntarism and emphasis upon individual will that is basic to existentialism. The similarity can be seen in the existentialist notion of encounter and Farrer's notion of apprehension. Buber's discussion of the I-thou relationship and Bultmann's focus on existential decision as the locus of the encounter between God and man portray knowing as an immediate encounter between two persons. Any third term such as language or analogy may serve as a catalyst for such an encounter, but the third term drops out when immediacy is attained. The relation of knower to known is a dyadic one. *Finite and Infinite* is written in the expectation that the use of particular analogies might bring the reader to a point where he will jump to the apprehension of what cannot be described, but can only be indicated. Direct apprehension is the goal of the essay.

In this quest for immediacy and for the jump to the apprehension, Farrer's epistemology is similar to that of Tillich. The difference lies in their respective paradigms of what it is to know or to meet another without mediation. For Tillich the paradigm is participation. One knows himself or another primarily by participating in that which is to be known. For Farrer immediacy arises in moments of encounter, in moments of apprehending another person or object. In both cases immediacy is the ideal and the goal, but the paradigmatic instance is different.

The encounter between wills is the prime model for interpersonal knowledge in this conception, but knowledge of impersonal objects is also dependent upon the jump for recognition. Words are never adequate; they are names for and indications toward the private experience of apprehension. Language is composed of words that function as tags applied to apprehensibles. To know is to accomodate grammar so as correctly to reflect or picture the relation of facts to each other in the world.[4] The world is made up of many entities that are related in complex ways. The task of systematizing knowledge is to build chains of analogical relations or complex propositions in order to reflect the ways in which these individuals are related.

Ontology. The basic picture of the world offered by this conception is one of an aggregate of individuals. Each individual is conceived as a point source of force or energy. The focus of this conception is on individuals interacting and colliding.

A consequence of this conception has been the sharp separation of the natural physical and even social environment from personal interaction. Knowledge of persons is distinguished from knowledge of things. Since knowing proceeds by analogy, a distinction is made between the application of the analogy of the self to other persons (the "problem of other minds") and a more generalized application to other things. Farrer has some perceptive insights about the human body in *Finite and Infinite,* but they are classified under the heading "Bodily bias of the will." The addition of the body is a step in the generalization of the substance formula from a description of the will to a description of the self. The body and the physical world are interpreted as environment for the will.

Tillich drew upon the procedure of the idealists in searching for the conditions of thinking, and this search led to universal categories that underlie the personal but which are not in themselves personal. In this second type, the point of departure is a description of the self as agent. Thus the personal will is perceived as a unit in a way that is not possible when the focus is on the intellect and its presuppositions.

The doctrine of God in the individualistic type emphasizes the model of the agent and the attribute of freedom. Farrer directs the reader toward the apprehension of God through the analogy of the unity of the self in its willing. This view of God as primarily will or agent is present in the work of Karl Barth. Barth's discussion of knowing as participation was mentioned in connection with the monistic type, but his doctrine of God[5] and parts of his doctrine of the creature[6] focus on the will and human freedom and reflect this second conception. Barth's doctrine of God is discussed under the perfections or attributes of divine freedom and divine loving. Even loving is interpreted as God turning toward man in his freedom. Freedom is the chief perfection. God's otherness is emphasized both in epistemology and in ethics. This freedom and distance from the human leads to descriptions of God as "wholly other." The basic model is that of the free agent.

Ethics. Strong emphasis is placed upon the freedom of the individual. Ethical claims are described in terms of commands or imperatives. R. M. Hare's discussion of ethical imperatives as commands or claims that are universalized, and the similar discussion of the divine command in Barth both exemplify this type.[7] The mode of ethical interaction that is appropriate to the I-thou encounter is that of command and response. The interaction is between conflicting wills. As in Bultmann's ethic of command and obedience, each situation is a call for a new decision. There is no teleology or attraction of the good, and no abstraction of principles that can be applied in several different situations. This results in a contextualism in which all continuity is denied between one context and the next. Contextualism is related to immediacy. There are no judgments to be made concerning the application of principle to situation. The situation provides the answer in the form of immediate intuition or command. Both the first and second types may be contextualistic.

A sharp distinction between nature and personal will often results in the claim that the natural order is ethically neutral. Deontological claims are stressed and naturalism is excluded from ethics. Or it might be claimed that values reside in persons, but not in the natural order.[8] A person is a center of intrinsic value and is to be valued as an end in himself and not for his participation in the good that manifests itself through him. Theological scrutiny of the Christian is focused on the person of Jesus or on his existential self-understanding rather than on his transparency to being or on the diffusion of the incarnation into the natural and social orders.

Freedom is the dominant value in the ethics of this second type. This is consonant with the attempt to view the natural order as neutral. Only persons are capable of freely deciding and of acting on those decisions. There seems to be a suspicion in some existentialist writing, for instance, that attractive values, physical constraints, or even psychological motives detract from personal freedom and autonomy and should be expunged as completely as possible from the moment of decision. Decision is a matter for the naked will. Farrer is more sophisticated here. He provides a subtle account and analysis of solicitation and response, bodily bias and motives, but he still maintains sheer volition as the final determinant between alternative courses of action.

The paradigm of command and obedience functions in discussions of sin and salvation also. Sin is interpreted primarily as disobedience and salvation is the redirection of the will in response to the divine command. Salvation does not mean reunion with God, but the congruence of the human will with the divine. This congruence or obedience is not something that is attained once and for all. It requires a new decision in each moment. Justification is central. God judges man to be acceptable even in his disobedience. Atonement is not a matter of redressing a balance or of effecting a subjective change, but it is a forensic decision, an act of will that is appropriate to the command-obedience motif.

The notion of conversion or *metanoia* is appropriate to this type. Sin is the result of the opposition of personal will to the good that is the will of God. Thus salvation consists in a change of will, a conversion, a turning around and moving in a different direction. Conversion is interpreted in the monistic type as change from a parochial perspective, a narrowness in which subordinate values are idolized, to a more comprehensive view. Conversion in the second type is interpreted as a turning around in one's tracks, a change of will and a new pattern of decision-making.

Kierkegaard's writings fall within this second type. His focus upon estrangement and upon the self's alienation from itself and from God might at first seem to be appropriately classed with Tillich. But one clue to the part-whole ontology of the first type was the lack of any convincing distinction between sin and finitude. Alienation was ontological as well as ethical. There could be no salvation that maintained individuality. In Kierkegaard the alienation and estrangement is ethical rather than metaphysical. Salvation is not reunion with God, but is the life of faith. One can be saved only by becoming an individual. Sin and dread are the sources of man's alienation from himself, his fellows, and God. This alienation is closely bound up with finitude but it is not identified with it. The kingdom of God for Kierkegaard would be a kingdom of individuals. In the eschatological extrapolation, individuality would be pronounced rather than obscured as it is for Tillich. The ethical distance that is lacking in Tillich's ontology is prominent in Kierkegaard's discussion of sin.

DISTANCE AND IMMEDIACY

A significant issue in the comparison of the three types set forth in this essay is the issue of mediation versus immediacy in knowing and acting. Both the monistic and individualistic types represent the ideal conditions of knowing and acting as immediate relations. Each of the finite conditions that mediate between subject and object in mundane existence is overcome or transcended at the level of the metaphysical ideal. Sociality and time are the two most important conditions that serve to mediate knowing and acting. Both of these conditions enter into the use of language. Thus a focus on the implicit theory of language in each type may serve to illumine the issue of mediation.

The chief difference between the conceptions of the monistic and individualistic types on the issue of mediation is represented by the presence or lack of distance within the metaphysical model. A purely monistic scheme lacks distance. All beings interpenetrate through their mutual participation in being. In a pluralistic conception, distance separates each entity from the others. No individuals interpenetrate. They exert force upon one another at collision or some point of interpersonal contact. Immediate encounters may still be sought within this second conception but they are portrayed as points of contact in a world in which the normal state is one of distance between entities. A brief discussion of some of the implications of this conception of distance and the immediate will precede the analysis of Farrer's philosophical theology.

In a monistic system distance is interpreted as estrangement and as distortion of true reality. It is not natural. Parts of a whole are united by their participation in a common ground. There is no distance between mother and infant at the earliest stages. Such distance as occurs is threatening. As the child develops a sense of "me" and "my," this distance becomes familiar and is tested and fully appropriated by some process of weaning and declaration of autonomy. The ontogeny of the infant is recapitulated in phylogeny as viewed from the history of ideas. The earliest portrayals of being in pre-Socratic philosophy sought to ground all experience in simple elements or forces. The Platonic doctrine rooted all experience in the ideas or forms and finally in the form of the good. In the Platonic and Neoplatonic schemes there were no distances. The divided line was a spectrum, as were the analogy of the cave and the chain of being. There are differences of degree along a spectrum, but there is no discontinuity.

Changes in social structure accompany and give rise to the development of ideas. The change in the structure of society at the end of the Middle Ages from feudal government to urban government, where former serfs were granted the privilege of citizenship, is coordinated with other conceptions of autonomy. It was in this period that nominalism was articulated as a philosophical position. Words and ideas were interpreted as names given by men to objects of perception and imagination. Men were conceived as agents who name the universe as they experience it. The emphasis shifted from intellect, from the purely passive perception of the ideas of reason, to the active naming and thus creating of the environment. The nominalism developed by Occam led to a conception of both God and man as primarily will. God's activity and decisions in creating and governing the world were stressed. Men had to do now not with a cosmic order, with a ground of being, but with a personal will who could be confronted. God was conceived as transcendent in the sense that he was omnipotent, but man and God could confront one another.

This change in social structure and the rise of voluntarism led to the possibility of Luther's intellectual and political break with Rome. Luther felt himself to be a person standing before God. In the face of the righteousness of God as one who decides and judges, the institutional and intellectual hierarchies lost their power to mediate. It was necessary for each individual to stand before God as sinner before his judge. The conflict and its reconciliation came through the encounter of the divine and human wills across a distance.

This conception of distance and its concomitant voluntarism allows for a radical doubt that was not possible before the development of a sense of self as autonomous. On the Platonic model of knowledge as participation and *anamnesis,* the radical doubt proposed by Descartes was impossible to conceive. In the Platonic scheme every man participates in and thus knows the forms, even though this knowledge may be cloudy or beyond simple recall. The process of learning becomes a process of recollecting that which has been obscured by the forgetfulness of this existence. But if an individual is in fact distinct from and distant from other beings, if there is discontinuity rather than a forgotten continuity in a common ground, solipsism becomes a possibility and a threat. Descartes's proposal could arise only when it was possible for him to conceive of himself as a thinking and willing being who could separate himself from the world around him.

The theory of the social contract is the analogue in political thought of a pluralistic metaphysics. Individuals who are autonomous are the fundamental entities. Society is to be explained and justified by the free and voluntary cooperation of these individuals. In the medieval world the social structure and hierarchy were prior to the individual. They mirrored the scale of being in nature and in the cosmos. In social-contract theory any structure or government must be justified by appeal to the free consent of individuals. This is parallel and analogous to the shift in the meaning of words from the realistic contention that they are rooted in the ideas or forms of Plato to the nominalistic contention that such words are tags applied by the voluntary activity of men. The locus of justification is shifted from the unified cosmos of ideas in God or the Good, to the wills of men acting individually. Unity is discovered not in the whole, but in the individual.

In the Cartesian conception the knower no longer participates in the being of the objects of his knowledge, except when that object is himself thinking. Radical doubt is possible and judgment is necessary. With the advent of distance and the autonomy of the knowing individual, judgment is necessary and error is possible.

Metaphysical pluralism has exhibited two images or approaches to the definition of finite substance. The basic atomic units have been treated either as impersonal units on the analogy of billiard balls or molecules of matter or they have been treated as persons and selves as in the voluntaristic tradition. When the impersonal is taken as the basic image for substance, the language of physics is primary. The second approach stems from the voluntarism of the late medieval nominalists and is more prevalent in the modern period. The basic substantial unit is treated as a self, a center of force, and finally as will. Descartes set the precedent and the problem that haunts all forms of this second type. That is the problem of separating and creating a dichotomy between persons and things. In the Cartesian division of the world into *res cogitans* and *res extensa,* such a dichotomy can be seen. Bridges must be built from the thinking self to other persons and to objects in his experience, even such objects as his own body. God's will was invoked by Descartes to form this bridge, but the dichotomy between persons and things is not so easily crossed. While the Cartesian invocation of divine fiat is a clear example of *deus ex machina,* it is significant in that some sort of voluntarism, a focus on will and agency whether divine or human, is necessary to bridge the distance between units in a pluralistic metaphysics where there is no recognition of a social fabric. It is not accidental that epistemology and ethics became the two major disciplines in much modern philosophy. Both involve the building of bridges from the autonomous individual to other persons and objects, the former in knowing and the latter in acting.

Immediacy is still sought and held to be the instance of real knowing in the individualistic conception. Clarity of vision is the model for clear and distinct ideas. The guarantee of certainty that accompanies the apprehension is similar to that of participation in the monistic type and functions as does the transparency of Tillich's symbol. It is the moment in which immediate contact is made with the object. In one case the immediacy is participation in a common ground and in the other it is the contact. There is no recognition of the temporal or social process involved in knowing or of problems of comparison and interpretation. For

Descartes the goal was immediate intuition, a dyadic relationship in which knower confronts known. Language might aid in arriving at that point, but only as a catalyst. Since there is no recognition of a social fabric, the will becomes essential to this kind of pluralism. Power to effect the encounter must be invested either in the knower or in the object of knowledge, and that power is conceived as will.

The most influential recent statement of a pluralistic metaphysics originating in a notion of substance conceived as self and primarily as will is existentialism. The world of the existentialist is composed of selves whose chief virtue and fate is their autonomy or freedom. At times these individuals attempt to deny this autonomy and to avoid decisions concerning their own destiny, but this is to drop below the level of authentic selfhood into the herd or *das Man* (Heidegger). Individuals are portrayed not only as autonomous but as fundamentally isolated and alone. They are cut off from other persons and from the world of nature at the crucial points of their own existence. The moment of autonomous decision is elevated as the model, descriptive and normative, for all experience. Freedom is the prime virtue. There is no portrayal of a social fabric but rather the dyadic contrast between indecision and heteronomy on the one hand and decision and autonomy on the other.

A consequence of the assertion of immediacy as the goal and justification of knowledge in both the monistic and individualistic types is the removal of the moment of knowing from criticism and public scrutiny. One is grasped by an authentic symbol. The saint or the symbol is, for Tillich, transparent to the ground of being. There is no ready process for public interpretation to distinguish between symbols that galvanize men and touch the depth emotions of a culture, leading to demonic results, and those which humanize men and culture. Moments of ecstasy and theonomy are self-authenticating. It is impossible then to subject them to mundane processes for adjudication of values.[9] Similarly, in the individualistic type the emphasis is placed upon the apprehension. The logical description that is a public matter is differentiated from the apprehension. There is no appeal beyond the apprehension.

> Misapprehension is an ultimate, since of apprehension there is no other evidence but apprehending, and misapprehension, by definition, appears to apprehend.[10]

Emphasis often appears to be placed on the fact of decision rather than the content. Here again there is no provision to distinguish for the purpose of making value judgments concerning the content of the decision. When the immediacy or ecstasy of interpersonal encounter or decision is taken as self-authenticating, it is removed from any interpretation or scrutiny as to its value. The use of the term *authentic* may lead to a romanticizing of decision or charisma that is neutral on the question of consequences.

A major concern of the existentialists has ostensibly been to overcome Cartesian dualism. The subject-object split that is attributed to Descartes is the archetypal heresy.[11] In spite of this rhetoric, however, existentialism is in principle Cartesian. The existentialists are in agreement with Descartes that the world is composed of many individuals, some of which are selves distinguished primarily by their volition. They also continue the sharp distinction between person and nature, between *res cogitans* and *res extensa,* that was drawn by Descartes. They part company with him in their proposal for overcoming the subject-object split and accounting for the interaction between the two *res.* Contemporary existentialists are no longer able to call upon divine fiat as did Descartes.[12] The connection must be made by individual wills in moments of decision and action. But the connection is still one of immediacy. It is still described in terms of encounter, of clarity and distinctness, of authenticity and a meeting of wills that overcomes distance.

This existential anthropology is adapted for theology with the notion of the word or revelation serving as the immediate contact. This contact occurs for the Christian in the encounter with Jesus Christ, with whom he is able to be contemporaneous in such a moment. This is not a historical encounter, mediated through centuries of history, but it is an existential contemporaneity that functions as a claim for decision and ignores distances of space, time, and social context.

Farrer's analysis of voluntary activity is differentiated and subtle. While many have focused on decision as the paradigmatic activity of will, Farrer focuses on the will as project.

> The moral struggle is the most evident instance of an act of will, because in it we are concerned with the choice of willing or not willing. But this is no reason for thinking that willing is restricted to the moral struggle; and the definition of will which we extract from an examination of that struggle does not suggest any such limitation. For it defines will simply as the self-actualizing potency of a project.[13]

The notion of project enables him to describe an act of will in its duration, and to speak of the ability of will to initiate a complex act that binds together its constituents into a unity. Farrer's account of the knowledge of God, however, and his discussion of knowing in general, center around the concept of apprehension. The apprehension is immediate. It cannot be held or mediated by language or social conventions. There is no appeal beyond the apprehension. It is this apprehension that functions in Farrer's epistemology in a manner similar to the notion of decision in the existentialists. Apprehension is the aim of *Finite and Infinite*. It can be aided, but not communicated, by the language that he chooses for the book. This apprehension that is aimed at is analogous to the existential moment of decision. It does not allow for propaedeutic nor does it lend itself to integration with the structures of one's thought and language after it has occurred. It is immediate and cannot be guaranteed by any structure that is designed to control it. It is this notion of apprehension that provides the strongest link between the individualistic immediacy of the existentialist notion of decision and the immediacy of Farrer's epistemology in *Finite and Infinite.*

ANALYSIS OF RATIONAL THEOLOGY: APPREHENSION

Apprehension is a key term for Farrer's work. It is a term rich with connotations that functions in somewhat the same way as *concern* does for Tillich. Tillich exploits the fact that *concern* may denote the subjective state or interest of an individual in a particular object or course of action and it may also refer to the object of that interest. *Apprehension* also contains this double reference, which is both subjective and objective. It is a term with visual connotations, but it is an act of a subject, not a passive reception of visual light. The result or end of a cognitive act may be referred to as an apprehension. To be apprehensive about something is to be seized or grasped with anxiety or anticipation about an object or event that may be imminent. Apprehension carries the sense of being grasped by something outside of oneself, even while it is also the name for a cognitive act of a subject. Like *concern, apprehension* refers to a volitional act as well as a state of being affected.

Farrer's conception of knowledge is based on the model of visual perception. In this regard, he stands within the tradition of Thomism, in which the goal of man is the vision of God. All knowledge is based upon some kind of apprehension of that which is known. To apprehend an object is to see it, or to encounter it. The truth or falsity of statements in human discourse is ultimately dependent upon the presence or absence of an apprehension of the object in question. The structure of an argument or a calculus is carefully laid out, and then recourse is had to experience in order to check the points at which the calculus touches down and to discover whether or not the experienceable difference implied by the argument may be apprehended at the point indicated. Language, especially metaphysical and theological language, has as its primary function that of description. It describes a direction and so indicates the locus of an apprehension, or it describes the form of an object and creates an image through which something new might be disclosed to the listener. Descriptive language is paradigmatic language, though it might range from the precise descriptions of natural science to the free description of poetry and of pictorial art. Farrer's own descriptive talents and inclinations led him into the aesthetic realm, though some of his methodological remarks suggest that the descriptive language of natural science is taken as his model. In either case, language is an instrument of perception. Its meaning is found in the image that it elicits in the mind of the hearer, and its truth or falsity depends upon the correspondence of this image with the reality of his experience. The realm of language and the images that it evokes and the realm of experience are independent. One may move back and forth from either realm to the other in order to check the correspondence of the image with that which is apprehended in experience, but they do not exercise mutual influence on each other.

Farrer's discussion of the nature of the apprehension and its place in the knowledge of God underwent considerable change between his initial presentation in *Finite and Infinite* and his freer description in *The Glass of Vision*.[14] The former work limits itself to the realm of rational theology and of man's natural knowledge of God, and the later book deals primarily with revealed images, but there is enough continuity in subject matter to preclude the relegation of one to Farrer's natural theology and the other to his theology of revelation with no common grounds for comparison. Much of the discussion in *The Glass of Vision* deals with man's natural knowledge of God and suggests a modification of the view of analogy and imagery that is set forth and employed in *Finite and Infinite*.[15]

The primary movement between the two works is that from the concept of a bare and immediate apprehension of the infinite to a recognition of the correlative character of knowledge, the impossibility of transcending the mediacy of images, and the necessary involvement of discourse in the act of apprehension. This movement reflects broader changes in British philosophy during that period. The move from logical positivism to ordinary language philosophy also stems from the recognition of the impossibility of a bare apprehension of a simple fact that might provide the basis for an ostensive definition. The epistemological shift from Wittgenstein's *Tractatus* to his *Philosophical Investigations* is parallel to the less dramatic shift from *Finite and Infinite* to *The Glass of Vision*. In the former work, Farrer is in conversation with the logical positivists; in the latter he has appropriated some of the insights of those who were attempting to chart the diverse and subtle distinctions that characterize ordinary language.

Many traces of the later view may be found in *Finite and Infinite,* especially in Farrer's descriptions of the will and of the self. In the course of these descriptions, the impossibility of leaving the analogies and images completely behind becomes clear, but the thrust of the discussion of method in *Finite and Infinite* is to separate the bare apprehension from the language by which we point to it and speak of it. Similarly, in *The Glass of Vision* the revealed images seem sometimes to serve only as occasions for the bare apprehension, but the correlative character of our knowledge of ourselves and knowledge of the other, and the necessary mediacy of the image and of discourse in the act of apprehension are more fully recognized and developed in this work.

Apprehension is a concept drawn from the visual realm and it is also an act. Standing within the Thomistic tradition, Farrer conceives of existence as act. Apprehension is not participation. It implies an object that is apprehended and a subject who apprehends. One apprehends an other and the distinction between subject and object is maintained. The Aristotelian distinction between primary and secondary causation enables Farrer to attribute all activity in human knowledge of God to God as the primary cause, and yet to avoid the identity of man's act with God's act of self-knowledge.

Existence is act. The apprehension of an object is on the lower end of a scale that rises in degrees of voluntariness to the conscious acts of will and intellect. The analysis in *Finite and Infinite* focuses on the will and on the creativity of conscious choice. At several points, however, Farrer mentions the parallel between the activity of will and intellect and the possibility of providing a similar analysis of intellectual acts. The distinction of will and intellect in the rational consciousness in contrast to the identity of the two at a level of implicit act below consciousness and at an ideal level of perfection forms the basis for one of the anthropological arguments for God in the final section of the book.

> Understanding and creation are rather distinct aspects of every fully human act, than different acts. Human activity, taken as a whole, is a response to what is believed to be the case; and contains the moments both of cognition and of enactment. . . . It remains, then, that perfect understanding is possible only to a creative mind, which enacts or makes that which it understands, and understands it in the making of it. Thus alone can the form of the object be possessed by the subject, for it becomes the form of the subject's acts.
>
> Conversely it may be shown that the perfect act of will, or of creativity, is possible only when the relation of will and understanding has been elevated to that of an identity between the two.[16]

In principle, an analysis of intellect parallel to that of will, which forms the foundation of Farrer's analysis of finite substance, is possible if one could adopt a detached standpoint from which to observe the activity of the intellect. In fact, it is difficult to reflect immediately upon an act of reflecting while it is possible to reflect upon acts of conscious choice. Intellect is interpreted as an extension of will. Farrer speaks of them as parallel because they form two sections of the scale of conscious activity and are united below the conscious level and in an ideal extrapolation (pp. 51, 295). Reflecting involves choice and the selectivity of object and these phenomena are present to us in reflection upon the highest activity of will. In *The Glass of Vision,* Farrer does focus on the activity of the intellect and there he uses much the same method as he has in his earlier description of the will. The activity is described by its governing form or pattern.

At the outset of the study in *Finite and Infinite* Farrer states his proposal to begin with analysis of rational theology and to reserve the dialectic for later consideration. An apprehension of the infinite is presupposed, and the aim is to describe and to set forth the implications of this apprehension. Farrer asserts that an analysis of the structure of theism may be carried out apart from the question of its truth or falsity. Rational theistic belief possesses a certain logic or structure, and this structure may be exhibited in a scientific manner, after which it may be studied by the believer and the nonbeliever alike (p. 5). The former may accept it and the latter reject it, but there should be no disagreement concerning the structure of the belief that they accept or reject. Assumptions and breaks in the argument will not be disguised, and the logic will be exhibited for all to approve.

This section of his analysis of rational theology provides an insight into Farrer's thought concerning language. Language in *Finite and Infinite* is scientific language.[17] Precise linguistic usage is able to produce a calculus, or a map of the structure of theistic belief. The structure of the belief is entirely independent of the ground in which it is rooted. This is very different from the interpretation of language as symbol in the monistic type, where the symbol participates in that which it symbolizes and one can only grasp or be grasped by the symbol by also participating. Here there is no complicity of the belief in the apprehension or of the apprehension in the belief. Farrer does not expect real disagreement to arise over the use of language. Such disagreement as might arise would be questions of clarification, which could be answered by attempts at further precision.

> The analytical part of philosophy ought to be a matter of agreement. . . . Our purpose, then, will be to separate the analysis of logic from the exercise of judgment so that we may have agreement in proceeding with the former.[18]

Words are names that are applied to objects of apprehension. The question of truth is raised at the point of apprehension or encounter. It is the question of the referent. There is no appeal beyond the apprehension.

> In so far as error is eliminated, terms do not stand between the object and ourselves: indeed such a view is only possible to a vicious conceptualism like Kant's, if it is right to accuse him of thinking that the meaning of a term was a creation of the mind and applied to the given. But it is not; a term in its real reference is a label tied to an apprehensible to mark it, and the confusion introduced by bad terminology is ultimately a confusion of apprehension, or rather of imagination with apprehension, of which deception, as we have already seen, there is no infallible preventive beforehand nor infallible check after it has occurred. Misapprehension is an ultimate, since of apprehension there is no other evidence but apprehending, and misapprehension, by definition, appears to apprehend. (P. 103)

Some may object that the term *God* has no referent. But the scientific structure of the belief in God may be exhibited in a manner that is understandable and agreeable to all. It is independent of the analyst and of the reality for which it makes claims.

Theology differs from the natural sciences in that the object with which it deals and the apprehension of that object are unique. While the sciences may construct genera and label data with terms that apply over classes of objects, this is not possible for theology. For this reason, direct discourse about the object of theology is impossible. The object can be named, but the name *God* has a unique referent, which is without meaning to someone who does not apprehend this referent. It can be described only by the use of analogy, by describing classes and objects that fence around the area of apprehension, narrowing down toward the object and pointing in the direction in which it may be apprehended. The function of language is to refer to apprehensibles and to direct the attention of others to a point at which they might share in the apprehension.

It is possible for two persons to apprehend the same object and to differ in their judgment concerning it. In theory this is not possible in monistic schemes. To perceive something is to participate in its being. To know the good is to do the good. It is impossible to know the good and to choose something else. Differences in judgment are ascribed to differences in participation and therefore in knowing. The metaphysics of the first type does not have a developed doctrine of the will in which acts of choice and of judgment can be interpreted. The result is that these acts are read as different degrees of participation along a scale of being and knowing.

Since the object of theology is unique, there can be no possibility of speaking of it with univocal terms. Instead, we are driven to the use of analogy.[19] We are not only driven to the use of analogy, but there exist analogical relations between certain things. Analogy does not obtain between terms but between things; it is an analogy of being.

> Analogy is a relation between objects, capable of being classed as a species of "likeness."[20]

It does not obtain between simples, but between complexes.[21] It is a likeness of structure, but it is not a likeness from which an identical characteristic can be abstracted. Two triangles are not analogous, but rather are identical in their triangularity.

Creation, the relation of the infinite to all finites, is a unique relation. Farrer describes several kinds of interfinite relations: substance-constituent, agency-interior effect, and operation-external effect, showing that none of them is identical with the finite-infinite relation. Each has aspects that point toward a description of the relation between finite and infinite, but each also has its defects. None of these relations can be abstracted from its concrete instances and used univocally to describe the finite-infinite relation.

> About that which is simply unique there can be no discourse; we can only repeat its name, say that it is itself and not any of the others. Where, however, analogy exists, it is possible to make significant comparisons which bring out for us and fix our appreciation of that with which these analogies are drawn. (P. 23)

The term *unique* that is applied to the finite-infinite relation is a term of positive value. It has been mentioned earlier and it will be stressed below that there is a correlation between the metaphysics of the individualistic type and the development of autonomy and a sense of individuality in the life of a person as there is a correlation between the metaphysics of monism and the experience of the infant seeking reunion with its mother. *Unique* is a term that stresses the distinctness of one individual over against others. Søren Kierkegaard confessed that he wrote only for that one individual who might possibly be struck by his individuality as it came through his writings. In a monistic framework terms stressing individuality and uniqueness are interpreted as estrangement and alienation and are located farther from the center of being in which all participate. But for this second type such terms carry thoroughly positive connotations.

The finite-infinite relation is unique, but it is not simple. If it were simple as well as unique there would be no way by which we could speak of it except by proper name.[22] But it is an existent, an activity, and therefore it has a certain structure. Existence is common to both finite and infinite. Farrer begins with an analysis of theistic belief, and thus with the theistic conviction that infinite substance exists. God is an existent who exists totally in himself. *Esse est operari:* to exist is to act (p. 28). The assertion of the existence of infinite substance implies that it is a center of activity and of the structure that this activity demands. God is *a se,* and his existence does not depend upon any structure outside of himself, so that his existence includes within it the structure of his activity.

Two points should be underscored concerning the program on which Farrer has embarked. (1) The object of the analysis, and that which determines its truth or falsity, is an apprehension. Farrer will find it necessary to employ analogical dialectic in order to direct attention to the locus of this apprehension, but the truth claim rests upon the recognition of the apprehension, and not upon the argument itself. (2) Existence is activity. The object of the pointing is not a simple idea or a point of reference, but it is a center of activity. It is only through the experience of the activity of the self that this object might be apprehended. This second point underlies Farrer's attempt to reconstruct the doctrine of substance. Substance is structured activity. It is apprehended in the structure of personal activity, in the will. The self, as the unity of a complex of acts of the will, is apprehended as an instance of finite substance. Through an examination of the activity of the will, the unity of an act is apprehended. An act is not simple. It is a complex structure binding together the complete process from the initial solicitation to the completed act. The self is a unity of acts in one character. This, then, becomes the paradigm of substance, and the only point at which genuine apprehension of finite substance is available.

God is the perfect existent who exists completely within himself. But where is perfection of existence or perfect activity to be sought? Activity is not a genus that can be abstracted from its several occurrences. Activity has modes, but it has neither attributes nor accidents. It cannot be separated into an abstracted form and a material substance. In order to discover the most perfect activity, then, we must look to its highest mode. Activity-as-such cannot be separated from the scale of activities or of the different modes of activity. The task that lies ahead is that of focusing on this scale, at the point at which it is available for observation, and of moving up the scale in the direction of highest activity.

Farrer rejects the *scala naturae* of classical Thomism because he is skeptical of the possibility of having sufficient insight into the mode of activity exercised by other creatures in order to construct this scale. The activity of others cannot be apprehended so directly as one apprehends his own. Farrer turns instead to the personal experience of conscious choice. He appeals to the recognition of an interior scale of increasing voluntary choice or activity. This has the advantage of being a scale along which an individual can slide in his own experience. The total spectrum is experienced by each person from the least voluntary acts that he authors to those of maximum choice. Our own voluntary conscious acts form a continous scale of ascent and descent, which increasingly realizes the forms of apprehension, rationality, and will (p. 45). Apprehension is the most passive on the scale of acts, rationality involves more activity on the part of the self, and will involves the highest. Thus it is to the conscious choice of the will that one must look in order to discover and to describe activity-as-such.

The character of a thing is to be sought in its highest mode. A metaphysical principle is here introduced that is of central importance for Farrer's method. If the character, or the governing pattern or form, of an act is to be found in the highest mode of activity, then knowledge of this mode will provide knowledge of the whole. It is not necessary to treat the entire scale equally and thus to take a poll or to investigate the statistical variation over the whole field of human activity. Rather, preference is given to the highest mode, in which the real character of the activity is revealed.

In his description of the will, Farrer admits that there are many lower activities of the will that are ensconced far below the realm that conscious reflection is able to penetrate, but it is not necessary to know these activities in order to understand fully the nature of the will.[23] The object of analysis, then, will be those acts of conscious choice which form the highest activity of the will.

> Acts of will constitute a rising and falling scale; not all are equally acts or equally will; to the lower levels we give other names, "desire," etc. The lower levels are opaque to our apprehension, because in them an explicitly rational act cannot reflect upon its own form. We are justified in using the highest and most intelligible as our clue to the nature of the lower; for it is the only clue we conceivably could have, and the scale is continuous.[24]

The use of a scale of nature at all is an element of Platonism that Farrer has appropriated from Augustine and Thomas. It is important, however, to note the modification he has made of that notion. He rejects the scale of nature as a scale of being, as the context in which all beings are set. He speaks of a scale of conscious acts within the volitional experience of an individual. The individual entity is the metaphysical unit. This unit is not ensconced on a certain rung in a scale of being. Rather, the scale is used to describe the character of this unit. Farrer's employment of a type of scale of nature is subordinate to his description of substance primarily as will. It is the notion of individual substance and the primacy of will in the description of that substance that establishes the character of his metaphysics, and not his adoption of the scale of nature as an aid in the description of that substance.

The interior scale provides direction, but there are two distinct movements that must be made in the approach to the apprehension of the infinite. The first is to rise to the height of the human scale, and the second is to move beyond that height to the apprehension of divine activity. There can be no continuity between finite and infinite being, so the ladder does not extend all the way. These two steps may be interpreted as parallel to the two major types of analogy in Thomism: proportion, which is a scalar rise, and proportionality, which Farrer interprets as a proportionate relation between four terms that enables one to jump off the scale to the divine activity.[25] Noesis and the activity of the will are considered to be parallel, so that, as there is no continuity of being between the finite and the infinite, so there is no continuity of the aspiration of the intellect or of the will with divine being. The goal of the finite is not to become, or to participate in, the infinite, but to apprehend or to enter into communion with God. The distinction between subject and object is maintained. It is this distinction and the discontinuity between finite and infinite and between knower and known that differentiate the monistic from the individualistic type.

Although the object of rational theology cannot be included in any genus and thus cannot be described univocally, it is possible to apply negative criteria in order more closely to circumscribe the locus of the apprehension. The three negative criteria of simplicity, self-sufficiency, and universality may be applied to the notion of activity-as-such.[26] These must not be viewed as positive attributes taken from knowledge of the finite and applied to the infinite. They are negative (noncomposite, independent, unrestricted).

The procedure for approaching the apprehension, then, is as follows. Negative criteria may be applied to the idea of plenitude of will and intellect that is approached in the movement up the interior scale of experience. These criteria circumscribe a lacuna in the direction to which the scale points. The analogical dialectic of rational theology is then employed in order to effect a jump to the recognition of the apprehension. With the analysis of finite substance and the employment of the dialectic, a ladder is built for the ascension that is no longer needed at the point of the apprehension.[27]

The next step is to establish the lower term of the analogy, or to apprehend finite substance. This apprehension is to be discovered through an examination of the activity of the self as the subject of its acts. Substance is not a logical concept according to Farrer, but an empirical one. Directly or indirectly, it is given by the senses. A substance is a thing; it presents itself as a unit, as a complex unit.

> What we mean by a "thing" is a complex of elements which in our experience holds together and "behaves" as a whole.[28]

The elements are individual sense impressions. The unit of substance is more than just an aggregate of these elements; it has a unity that binds them together. It has the unity of an organism, or of a structured activity or behavior. In canvassing the field of experience for evidence of substance, something must be sought that presents itself as a unit, as an "other" over against the self.

The issue that underlies Farrer's attempt at a reconstruction of substance is that of unity. A unit of substance is a unit that is indivisible, from which neither accident nor attribute can be abstracted, and that is an existent, not a simple element of sense perception. Farrer finds the paradigm of this unity in the structure of an act. Activity unites the several elements involved in intention, initiation, and completion of the act. It is the unity that is observed in the act of coming to a decision or of the solution of a problem by the intellect. It has a structure, and it has a direction, but it cannot be subdivided into parts. By taking activity and the organic model as the paradigm of unity, Farrer avoids the competition between parts in any mechanical system. When the individual mechanical parts are each viewed as basic units, real unity of the whole is impossible. The most that can be constructed is a composite machine. In the organic model, however, the unit is taken to be the complete act and no division can be made in that unit.

Farrer holds that the only direct experience of complex unity is the experience of "interior psychic connection," or the experience of unity in the structure of activity of the will or the intellect. This unity of personal act becomes the model through which substance is apprehended. Onto the elements of data that are presented by the senses, "we project some vague analogy from our experience of interior psychic connection" (p. 67). The unity of activity is seen through comparison with the self. It is viewed as parallel to the self with respect to the question of the one and the many. With the self as the standard unit, this other is judged to be a unity.

> I treat the thing as an "other" over against "me," and though I do not call myself a "thing" or the thing a "self," I do erect a pseudo-genus of which "thing" and "self" are species. (Ibid.)

Things and selves are both regarded as bundles of which activity is the unifying principle.

This discussion of the perception of substance as an "other" over against the self provides a suggestion of the description of knowledge as correlative that appears more clearly in Farrer's treatment of the will and of the self. His analysis of rational theology suggests that the apprehension of the infinite is a bare apprehension that stands apart from all of the analogies used to point to it. When he comes to describe what the apprehension of another must be, however, he does it by reference to the self.

Farrer's short discussion of language in his prolegomena to the analysis of substance provides a good instance of the view of language to be found in this second type. Language is inadequate to and entirely separate from the level of apprehension. As noted above, analogy obtains between things and not between terms. Language is a conventional response that functions primarily to direct the attention of another in preparation for an apprehension, or to direct one's own imagination. The act of apprehension involves response on the part of the organism that apprehends, and language is a conventionalization of this response among humans. Words are labels that are ascribed to apprehensibles, or ejaculations that accompany the apprehension. They are to be checked by reference to the apprehension. In his discussion with the positivists, Farrer accepts the criterion of "experienceable difference" by which to judge the meaning of language, but he defines experienceable difference more broadly than most of the current formulations of the verification principle: "differences such that they can be appreciated by us, and such that there is appropriate to them a scale of behavior-reactions *other* than linguistic (conventional) reactions" (p. 74).

The inadequacy of this concept of language lies in the attempt at complete separation of the realm of language from the realm of the real or from the level of the apprehension of the real. Language is scientific language. The model is that of a calculus with constants, variables, and operators, which is totally distinct from the problems for which it is employed. Empirical data may be substituted for the variables and the operators, and the result that is obtained may be interpreted in terms of the original data, but the process is completely within the calculus. Similarly, the responses of an organism to its environment are frozen in the conventions of language and must be removed from these conventions in order to count once again as real responses.

The shadow of logical atomism is present in this analysis. Words are tags that are applied to apprehensibles. Speech is a manipulation of these tags in order to refer another to the apprehension on which the tag originally was placed. As the words are initially ejaculatory responses, so the function of language is to point. There is a certain correspondence between words and apprehensibles. Farrer would not admit to a rigid one-to-one correspondence such that an ordering of the language would provide a picture of reality, as was attempted by the early Russell and the early Wittgenstein. He views words as less dependable than this. They are inadequate to describe the objects of apprehension, since they cease to be proper names and become words only when several apprehensibles have been subsumed under one convention and a genus is formed.

Thinkers of both the monistic and individualistic types interpret language as inadequate to reality because they see true knowledge as an immediate relation between subject and object. In the first type the paradigm of this relation is the mystic's union with and participation in the object of his knowing, which becomes a vehicle for his participation in the whole, even if the object at hand is only the flower in the crannied wall. In the second type the paradigm is person-to-person encounter and language at its most authentic functions only as address or as proper name, which is extended to impersonal things as ostensive definition. This is interesting material for reflection in a day when many segments of the culture are once again proclaiming the inadequacy of language and extolling the nonverbal experience as well as new and newly adapted forms of mystical participation and artificial methods of simulating immediacy.

The program on which Farrer has embarked, and his aim in the analysis of will and of the self, is to direct the apprehension of the reader to the unity of substance. His method is that of analogical dialectic. In caricature, this method proceeds by describing the general area, limiting it by negative criteria, pointing the direction with the interior scale, and bringing to bear any analogy that will aid in the jump to the apprehension.

> And the purpose of the whole is that the listener may grasp the underlying dynamism and jump to the apprehension of X itself. (P. 83)

Discourse is mediate while the apprehension is immediate. Farrer criticizes Hegel for attempting to eliminate all analogy and to rest in calm possession of the truth (p. 84). The elimination of analogy is the goal of natural science, but it is impossible in a description of the unique, of that which cannot be subsumed under genera. Although Farrer does not want to allow the possiblility of the elimination of analogy in description or even in conception, he does assert an immediacy in perception or apprehension.

> All our rational knowledge of God reduces, therefore, to the knowledge of such a being as the creative agent of effects. This cannot mean, as we have seen, that our knowledge is simply mediate; we must have direct awareness of the activity, as well as of the effects, and of the agent so far as implicit in the activity. (P. 61)

This level provides a channel of immediate commerce with reality. The relative (and the ethical) is left behind for rest in calm apprehension of the truth. This is a case in which his theory is inadequate to account for his own subtle powers of description.

EXAMINATION OF FINITE SUBSTANCE: THE SELF AS WILL

The voluntarism that is present in the examination of finite substance in *Finite and Infinite* becomes more pronounced in Farrer's later work.[29] In *Faith and Speculation* (1967) he distinguishes the voluntarism of theism from the metaphysics of the monistic type in which the finite parts are grounded in the whole.

> The substance of theistic thought or reflection lies in the assertion of a higher analogue to rational will as primary determinator of all finite existence; and to wrestle with the problems which arise from such an assertion is to wrestle with the difficulties inherent in theism as such. And what is the evasive alternative? It is the pretence of settling the relatedness of finites to a divine ground without bringing into play the substantive theistic idea. It is very natural that so evasive a proceeding should prove vacuous. It is simply to be set aside as an unprofitable deviation, not dressed up as the dialectical opposite of the straight path from which it deviates.[30]

And central to the whole development (of theistic reflection) from start to finish is that voluntaristic account of deity which is so irredeemably analogical.[31]

Farrer's description of the self as will in *Finite and Infinite* is more subtle than his own statement of method can account for. It was noted above that his description of analogy as an aid in attaining immediate apprehension ignores complicity of the knower with the language he uses and with the social character of the apprehension. Farrer's own description of the will illumines this complicity at points. A theory of language that accounts for his own description would move toward a position similar to that outlined in the next chapter.[32]

Voluntarism is clearly at the core of *Finite and Infinite*, though it is stressed even more fully later. As mentioned above, this voluntaristic view of the self is correlated with an articulation of the experience of autonomy, of the self interpreted as one who chooses, who understands himself as an agent, a center of force over against other selves. It is based on a phenomenological description of experiences of over-againstness, of confronting other persons or things as "others" over against which we stand. This is the experience that is fundamental to the descriptions of the individualistic type.

Farrer begins his search for the apprehension of complex unity in the self, which provides the paradigm, and the only instance that is available for direct apprehension, of finite substance. The object of this search is the real connection, the *geistiges Band* that binds the self together. Farrer is appealing to the recognition that, in intercourse with others, the other is seen as a unit over against the self. Neither the self nor the other can be prescinded from this experience without changing the character of the experience or losing the meaning of that which is prescinded. I enter into experience as a self, and I recognize this self as a unit in contrast to other objects of my experience. Farrer is asking the reader to focus upon this experience and to attempt to discover wherein lies the bond of this unity.

He employs visual or pictorial images in his description of the activity of the will and he suggests that the will itself perceives the structure of its act and of its future project in a manner that might best be described in visual terms. Will is defined as the potency of an effect.[33] Several images are employed to characterize the will: that of a moral struggle in which the will is one participant alongside desire and habit, a project that creates a form stretching into the future but lacking material content, or a sleeping animal that is stimulated into action or is solicited by a project or a goal. Each of these is seen to be somewhat inadequate and is therefore rejected. The fact that the image is inadequate, however, does not mean that it is left behind.

Farrer's actual description of the nature of voluntary activity is more subtle than the account he has give of the function of language in apprehension would lead one to expect. He claims that analogy is employed to indicate and to circumscribe an apprehension, to which the language will never be adequate, and to enable the perceiver to leap beyond the language to the bare apprehension itself. But it might be more correct to say that we have in Farrer's description not analogy at all, but rather image and metaphor. The description does not negate itself or become transparent to the apprehension. The description remains, and it portrays something. It not only indicates, but it sketches.

Farrer begins by outlining the analogical dialectic, with its ideal of pure immediacy. The truth or falsity of the description is said to depend upon the immediacy of the apprehension.

> The test is, whether such experience is forthcoming or not, or rather, whether we have acquaintance with its object. If we have, it is enough, whether this account of the mode of apprehension is proper, or some other. On our principle, we shall expect the object to be far less obscure than the act by which it is apprehended. (P. 108)

But the images and metaphors that he employs do not negate themselves before the apprehension. Instead they serve, with all of their imaginal content, a mediative and interpretive function. Toward the close of his analysis of the will, when this function has become clear, Farrer says:

> That, then, of which we hoped to have a clear apprehension without analogic mediation, that which was to be our clue to its darker analogues, will shine before all with a qualified clarity. (P. 144)

It would take a social conception of language and interpretation to account for the mediating function of the images and metaphors that Farrer employs and for the "qualified clarity" with which they shine. Such a conception will be set forth in connection with the third type.

The purpose of the description is to point to something that is apprehended as a unity. The unity that Farrer discovers in the act of the will is described in figurative terms, as if it were a spatial map or pattern of the act.

> There is, then, an event of which we can say, that it exists or occurs *qua* being a unit of a certain extension and pattern. This event is an event which is willed; and this extension and pattern have a privileged metaphysical position relatively to other extensions or patterns that may be found within, or overlapping into, the event; for they have a privileged relation to the existence of the event. (P. 121)

One of the most impressive phases of Farrer's analysis is his development of the correlation of solicitation and response. Farrer is attempting to show that will and desire are not really opposites, but are correlative aspects of one act.

> The nature of interest (i.e. interestingness) is to solicit activity; the nature of the will is to respond to the solicitation of interest. Neither is intelligible without its correlative. . . . There is indeed no solicitation without some tentatives toward positive response, for unless the besieger has some friends within the fortress, there is no bother made even about his non-admittance. (Pp. 136-37)

Will responds to interest. Solicitation is tentative response.
These are not two different events.

> solicitation is not an event in what solicits (unmoved mover) but
> in that which is solicited (the moved). Solicitedness, not solicita-
> tion, is the event, and is a state of tentative response or re-
> sponses rather, while that to which solicitation solicits, viz.
> adequate response in the enactment of the project which inter-
> ests us, puts an end to solicitation itself. (P. 137)

Stimulus and cause are images that must here be used correlatively. Either one alone gives a reductionist picture of
the activity of the will. Both stimulus and cause are two
sides of the same event, just as command and response are
correlated.

A similar dialectic is employed in the description of the
object of the will (p. 153). The basis of the will's action is not
adequately described as either deontological or teleological.
The object of the will that solicits the action can be seen
either as the project of the future act or as the completed act
that is the entity willed. This dialectic is not transcended,
but it forms the description. Similarly, in Farrer's discussion
of freedom, the notion of freedom as unfettered and un-
obstructed action after the fashion of *creatio ex nihilo,* in
which the existence of any given condition implies a reduction of freedom, must be set over against a concept of freedom to choose one or another of several given alternatives,
or of freedom to act upon sufficient evidence. And finally,
the governing dialectic is that of the one and the many in
the search for unity of the act.

The result of these descriptions is that the apprehension
is not a bare apprehension that stands beyond the dialectic
of the several analogues, but it is perceived only through
the analogues. Farrer's description of the will demonstrates
his recognition of this point, but his analysis of rational
theology and of the significance of images and of language
denies it.

Farrer maintains not only a correlation between the various analogues involved in the dialectical description of the will, but also a correlation and an analogical relation between the highest level of the will and each lower level. His concept of the internal scale of will-acts leads him to assert that his analysis of the self, which focuses on only a small part of the self's activity, that of conscious choice, is valid for the apprehension of the unity of the whole self. Thus he is concerned not to identify the self with a residuum that lies below all of our conscious acts and that is thus supposed to be in principle out of the reach of reason. Likewise he is concerned not to speak of a transcendent self that exists beyond all of our conscious acts and is similarly unobtainable by reason. He sets his method over against those who assert that the will is ensconced in the shadows of the unconscious and is thus essentially unintelligible.

> You may take the unintelligible as your standard of what will is, and add its occasional intelligibility as an "accident," or you may take the intelligible as your clue to its nature, and treat the "unintelligible" examples as not the substratum of the intelligible stripped of its intelligible aspects (which would be to think nothing) but as something analogous to the complete intelligible substance. (P. 143)

Farrer investigates first the body as a possible unifying principle for the activity of the self, and next the pattern or project that governs the various activities of the will. The second of these alternatives is obviously not a single unity, since no finite being possesses the purity of heart to will one thing, but is rather a pattern of various project units. In accord with his consideration of existence as activity, Farrer conceptualizes the relation of the body to the will as a constraint upon the pattern of its activity. The will must be construed as simultaneously enacting two patterns. The first is a cyclic and constant pattern that meets the biological needs of the organism in the face of the environment but does not require constant attention. On top of this vital pattern of activity is superimposed the superpattern of particular acts. The vital pattern provides the context and the scope within which the will forms the superpattern, but it does not determine that pattern directly. In acts of conscious choice, the will operates the superpattern on the basis of the vital pattern of the organism. The unity of the self that is given by the body is then perceived to be the dominant formal pattern that governs this activity. It is not a simple unity of the superpattern, but rather a series of projects that are united in the activity of the will. This superpattern of projects is united in two ways:

> (a) in the projects we explicitly or implicitly entertain together at any one time, (b) in the analogy or similarity of policy between our projects at several different times throughout life. (P. 190)

Farrer speaks of character as the policy of choice. It is an active belief in our own practical judgments of the past. No self is without a character. There can be no "intuitive" self, a self with direct intuition of the objects of practical judgment.

> We cannot hope for a blinding flash of clarity by which the single object should of itself alone fully illuminate the understanding. We must build on our previous judgments (that is our acts *qua* rational) and construct a system of practical belief which, we hope, more and more approximates to a true response to the real nature of things. (P. 194)

In the face of this analysis it is difficult to understand why Farrer seems to hope for such a blinding flash of clarity in the realm of cognitive apprehension. His analysis of the will and of the practical reason shows a recognition of the mediacy in our relation to objects with which we are confronted, but this is not the case in the realm of the intellect. The parallel that he wants to maintain throughout between the activity of the will and that of the intellect seems to be compromised at this point.

After his analysis of the starting-point of the will (body) and its aim (project), Farrer turns to look at the background from which the choice is made. How does the concentration

of the forces of the memory contribute to the unity of the
self in act? As there is a scale of will-acts, there is also a scale
of concentration ranging from the least rational to the most
rational pole. But concentration and active choice are correlative. They are aspects of a single process.

> To choose a project we must concentrate the background, and,
> conversely, to concentrate the background we must have the
> (formation and) choice of a project in view. (P. 203)

Thus there is always some concentration of mnemic matter
that sets the orientation of the self toward possible objects.
This activity of concentration may exist at a very low level,
but it is never absent. The self is never fully passive to its
object, but always goes forth along a certain path to meet it.
This activity of the self is a part of the act of the will and
thus excludes the possibility of the will's being determined
solely by its object. So also with the intellect in matters of
cognitive apprehension.

From a description of the background of the will's choosing, of its starting point and its aim, Farrer turns to the
question of the agent. What is the *efficiens* of the act? Existence is activity and so the agent itself is a concentration of
act. It is "the system of act to which the new act stands
immediately related" (p. 214). This act-situation is constituted by acts that directly precede the new one and by those
acts which are contemporaneous with it. Farrer appeals
here to a dialectic of serial unity and concentration. The self
is a series of acts that follow upon one another in temporal
sequence, and yet it must also be seen as focused in the
present through the concentration of completed acts and
future projects. The dialectic of the one and the many
applies to this view of the self as concentration and as continuous serial act.

It appears as if the self is the victim of reductionism at this
point. Farrer is not suggesting that his description of the
agent in the concentration of act be taken as the locus of the
unity of the self. Each of these aspects of unity, in body, in

project, and in concentration, is inadequate, but they are to be taken together as mutually correcting analogies.

> The unity-in-plurality which will actualizes cannot be exhibited by any scheme of terms and relations, but only be intuited *in re*. (P. 219)

The unity of the self must not be limited to any of these elements within the analysis, but it must be a unity that is apprehended in all its aspects. The act of analysis of the activity of the self that Farrer has undertaken rules out the possibility of apprehension of the unity, but this analysis may prepare the way for such an apprehension outside of the analysis. A move must be made beyond the dialectical analysis to the intuition. Any number of dialectical formulations could be employed in order to point to this unity, but each formulation will include an agent, something with which he is concerned, and the act in which he deals with this thing. But each formulation will have as its purpose the direction of the attention of the perceiver to the locus of the apprehension.

In his generalization of the substance-formula from a description of the apprehension of the unity of the self to a description of the apprehension of substance generally, or of "thinghood," Farrer becomes more explicit concerning the correlative character of knowledge of the other and of the self:

> Now it is suggested that the concrete datum is not of an object having the form, but of the interaction-event, and that it is from this that the anomalous abstraction is made; and then, perhaps, never without the help of analogy from our own substantial being. (P. 232)

Farrer attempts to illustrate this by appeal to the conception of a common or basic sense.[34] The point is not that there exists such a sense that lies under or beyond the five senses, but rather that the apprehension of "thinghood" or of an other is not arrived at by the combination of elements of data from each of the particular senses. Perception is not only of color, extension, solidity, and the like, with the combination and unity of these elements into a "thing" being left up to the resources of the mind. Rather, there is a basic perception of substance as something that is other than the self and with which the self interacts.

The unity of substance is to be found in the unity of operation and not in spatial boundaries. We are aware not only of "thinghood" but of things, and for this awareness the apprehension of another self, or a center of activity, is paradigmatic. The self organizes and unites a multiplicity of subordinate forms, but it possesses a unity of operation that is recognizable to us. In the case of lower forms of life and of inanimate objects it may not always be possible to locate the divisions exactly and to discriminate between the various units of activity. The units are present, however.

Substance is known through the interaction with an other, in the case of things as well as selves, since all existents are structures of activity. In this interaction we come to distinguish between operations and patterns of activity, and thus to distinguish individuals. The perceiver is ensconced in a world of activity with which he is in constant interaction. There is now no possibility of conceiving him as a passive receiver of impressions from the external world. Recognition must be given to his participation in the events of perception and to the interpretation that is required of him in order to distinguish between governing and subordinate units of operation. The apprehension is neither bare nor immediate. Knowledge cannot now be understood with reference to the model of apprehension or of visual perception alone, but it also demands a cognitive moment of interpretation. It was this insight that led Charles Sanders Peirce and Josiah Royce to the metaphysics of community, which constitutes the subject of the next chapter.

There is a discursive moment in the act of knowing. Discourse or thinking takes time and involves the selectivity and rejection of perceptive data from a number of different spatial and temporal standpoints. Language cannot be viewed only as a set of conventional tags that are applied to the objects of apprehensions. The role of language in discourse must be recognized as an aspect of the perception-interpretation event, without which knowing would not occur. Language is not only a matter of acknowledgment or of ejaculatory response to the apprehension, but it is a discursive response. In language the perceiver takes up and masters the perceptual data rather than being mastered by them.

The role of the intellect in interpretation and the dimension of time involved in the act of knowing are minimized by Farrer. The social character of language is ignored completely. It is this neglect that enables him to treat language as a secondary phenomenon and to speak of the apprehension beyond the analogues. Here in his description of knowledge of other substances, however, is a recognition of the correlative character of knowledge. This character of knowing and of language cannot consistently be accounted for within the framework of the individualistic type. Recognition of the social and temporal character of language and thus of selves demands a metaphysics that begins with the communal character of existence rather than with the isolated individual.

THE DIALECTIC OF RATIONAL THEOLOGY: COSMOLOGICAL

In his execution of the dialectic Farrer treats a number of distinctions within the finite order as broken images of the infinite. Apprehension of the infinite is through the image of finite substance and is correlative with the apprehension of the finite. These broken images are not symbols that participate in the ground of the infinite and that become transparent to that ground as in the monistic type. They are images of something that is other than they rather than of

something of which they are parts. The dialectical proofs
that Farrer employs are designed to aid as catalysts for correlative awareness of finite and infinite. They embody a
process of reflection upon this awareness and of discursive
reason that clarifies and criticizes this awareness. They emphasize the relation of creator to creature because this
image conveys the discontinuity between finite and infinite
that is not present in images such as part/whole and being/
ground of being.

> There is nothing dialectical so far; our actual implicit awareness
> of God's creative action in the finite is made explicit by a train of
> reasoning which analyses the finite by an implicit comparison
> with God, condemns it as composite by the same implicit com-
> parison, and judges the composite to be dependent by the im-
> plicit awareness that this compositeness is the effect of a divine
> creation, placing a qualified and finitised image of the divine
> being outside God.
>   True dialectic begins when we give reasons for the validity of
> the "why" question.[35]

Each of the dialectical proofs considered by Farrer is a
form of the cosmological argument. The cosmological argument emphasizes the discontinuity between finite and infinite, while the ontological argument emphasizes the continuity. From a distinction within the finite, the attempt is
made to show that the coexistence of the elements distinguished, in the manner in which they do coexist, is unintelligible apart from the existence of an infinite ground of
such a coexistence (p. 262). Of primary importance is the
argument from the distinction between essence and existence in finite substance. This is the basic distinction in the
finite realm and it provides the paradigm for, and even the
condition of, each of the other demonstrations. The others
employ distinctions that might be more easily recognized,
but that ultimately lead back to the distinction between essence and existence.
  Farrer divides the proofs into the anthropological and
the "usiological" (a term of Farrer's coinage, from *ovsia* [be-

ing or essence]), according as they begin from the substance of the self or from a generalized notion of finite substance. Since the self is the only substance of which direct apprehension is possible, and all knowledge of other substance involves generalization from the self, these are the only two possible points of departure. There is also a cross-division of the proofs into immanental and transcendental. The former presupposes the existence of one of the distinguished elements in the finite order and then attributes the addition of the second element to intervention from beyond the finite. This is philosophically absurd because neither of the elements can be presupposed without the other. While essence and existence may be distinguished in correlation with one another, it is impossible to conceive of essence as a form to which existence is added, or of existence that is subsequently shaped by essence. The transcendental forms of the proofs begin from the composite existence of both of the elements that have been distinguished, and argue that this composition demands a ground that transcends the finite. Neither of these forms provides a syllogistic argument. They are analogical illustrations that are designed to clarify the implicit awareness of the infinite through finite substance. They provide illustrations and occasions for reflecting upon the correlative apprehension of finite and infinite, and for selecting those aspects of finite substance which best clarify this apprehension and which best serve in analogical description of the infinite.

The arguments from the generalized notion of finite substance (usiological arguments) are divided into those which proceed from the finitude of finite being (i.e., from the distinction of essence and existence or of activity and its modes) and those which proceed from substantial relations within the finite order. Each argument is formally refuted as a philosophical argument and materially justified as an analogical description. The proofs, as arguments, pretend to a process of elimination: since the coexistence of essence and existence in finite substance is not intelligible by itself, then one of the elements must have been added by intervention from outside of the finite realm, or the coexistence of these two elements requires a ground beyond the finite. This is, however, to suppose that the alternatives that we conceive form an exhaustive set. But the set of known finite substantial relations cannot be taken as exhaustive when the object of the search is a unique relation that cannot adequately be expressed by any of the finite relations.

The anthropological arguments take their departure from the notion of the interior scale and from its relation to human conditions or limitations. Existence of the various modes of voluntariness in acts of the will and in the modes of apprehension by the intellect is contrasted with the ideas of sheer creativity and sheer noesis.

> Reason is bound up with the idea of perfect apprehension. . . . For knowledge must be defined as the intellectual vision of what is; and since our acts do not achieve this, they are knowledge by their approximation to, or more exactly their participation in, knowledge. But this involves at least the belief that perfect apprehension is thinkable, and intrinsically possible, though not for us. (P. 291)

Here the visual conception of knowledge is clearly stated by Farrer. The purpose of this imagery is to contrast the brokenness and obscurity of human knowing with the perfection of angelic and divine knowing. Farrer speaks of acts of human cognition as acts "in which sheer apprehension is filtered by the gross instruments of sense and thought that we are forced to use" (p. 288). Bare apprehension of the infinite is not attainable through the analogical dialectic, but the notion of perfect knowledge as bare apprehension continues to lie behind the imagery. This knowledge is not possible in the finite state, but behind the broken images of finite substance and the distortion of the senses lies the unbroken beam of sheer noesis. Sheer noesis demands sheer creativity. Will and understanding are united in infinite act. The mutual externality of will and understanding in the creature is due to its imperfection. This imperfection or disunity acts as a defective lens to break and to refract the beam of apprehension.

Royce, following Peirce, denied that perfect apprehension was possible. Ideal knowledge cannot be conceived in terms of immediate vision or encounter. Knowledge is human knowledge. There is no access to what knowing could possibly mean other than through human knowledge. And knowing involves interpretation and mediation. This moment of interpretation is not a defect that must be ascribed to the poverty of finitude. It is an aspect of the process of knowing and must be accounted for by any analysis that purports to illumine that process.

Farrer's visual imagery ignores the discursive or the temporal moments in knowing. Apprehension remains the paradigm. The aim is to adopt a position from which the object may be most clearly seen. Analogical description is employed to aid in the approach to this view, though perfect apprehension will never be reached. Language continues to function by pointing. The descriptive use of language in which images retain their original meanings and provide multiple pictures and sketches of an object, an art well exemplified in Farrer's own descriptions of the will and of the self, is not recognized here. The image of the beam that is refracted and distorted by the senses and by finite substance does not accurately portray the activity of the knower in knowing. To begin from the notion of sheer apprehension and discuss its limitations in human knowing is to ignore the correlative moment that Farrer has portrayed in his discussions of solicitation and response and of the character of the self. Human knowing is not adequately described by sheer apprehension nor by the apprehension of a broken beam. It involves the perception of images from a multiplicity of standpoints and the interpretation and ordering of that which is perceived. It is a development of this notion of interpretation that provides the starting point for the metaphysics of community set forth by Josiah Royce.

For a consideration of Farrer's recognition of this issue, and his abandonment of the notion of the bare apprehension, let us briefly attend to his discussion of the imagination in *The Glass of Vision*. While he moves in that work from the notion of apprehension to that of the image, he still does not address the problem of interpretation that will lead us into the third type.

THE GLASS OF VISION: IMAGINATION AND DISCOURSE

In *The Glass of Vision* the primary analogy for the knowing intellect is still that of the eye, as the title suggests. The discussion of analogy and image in this work, however, emphasizes the descriptive function of thought and language as opposed to the indicative function that is dominant in *Finite and Infinite*. The metaphysician describes mysteries, and he is able to point only to his imaginative description. There is no reference to a beam of sheer apprehension that stands behind the mysteries or behind the metaphysician's description. Emphasis is placed much more on the relative and correlative character of human knowing than was the case in the earlier work. Paradigmatic language is not now scientific language, but aesthetic language. Indeed, metaphysics is explicitly distinguished from the natural sciences by its concern with mysteries as opposed to the problems of the sciences. The activity of thinking is given consideration as well as seeing, and discourse is recognized as a necessary aspect of the act of knowing.

The investigation is here focused on the intellect rather than on the will as in *Finite and Infinite*. Although much the same process is employed in the analysis, particularly the principle of the hierarchical character of human knowledge, the model of an interaction of wills is not present and thus is not transferred to the description of the intellect. The analysis of the confrontation of the will by the object in *Finite and Infinite* provides a model that reinforces the parallel between an object presented to the intellect and a visual object presented directly to the eye. This model is not present in *The Glass of Vision*, and in fact Farrer explicitly rejects the direct and immediate form of knowledge.[36] The process of knowing is much more indirect and descriptive.

The eight lectures of *The Glass of Vision* may be divided into three sections. The first two lectures are devoted to the establishment of a distinction between the natural and the supernatural, and to the maintenance of the distinction between natural reason and supernatural revelation, while the third initiates the discussion of inspiration and of the supernaturalization of images in revelation. Natural reason and supernatural revelation are to be distinguished as man's action and God's action by the supernaturalizing of nature, or the working of effects through second causes, which effects do not arise from the natural powers of those causes. Following this introductory material, Farrer considers issues of natural theology and of revealed theology, the latter involving him in an inquiry into the inspiration and communication of images.

The idea of the supernatural, as Farrer describes it, is of "a finite agent exceeding his natural powers by higher assistance" (p. 14). There is a hierarchy of human acts and self-knowledge has an hierarchical structure. We know ourselves by our upper limits, or by the governing operation of our activity. This is familiar doctrine after our investigation of *Finite and Infinite*. Since we know our upper limits, we are able to distinguish the supernatural from the natural, and to avoid confusing it with the preternatural, which lies below the level of consciousness. The supernatural is never discontinuous with the natural; the finite does not exclude the infinite as one finite excludes an incompatible finite (as blueness excludes redness or as the presence of molecules of a gas excludes a vacuum). Rather, God as first cause works effects through second causes, which are not attainable by the natural powers of those causes. This employment of the Aristotelian distinction between primary and second-

ary causation enables Farrer to speak of the two-sided nature of human existence and experience. The shadow of
divine agency is present in all human activity.

> The total fact is never myself alone, not even myself with the
> world for its environment, but always my world-environed self,
> *and God*. (P. 28; original emphasis)

This is a statement of the correlative character of the experience of the finite and the infinite. Farrer interprets this
experience in terms of the scheme of primary and secondary causation, but the experience is prior (logically, though
perhaps not temporally) to the interpretation.

Supernatural revelation bestows an apprehension of divine mysteries that are inaccessible to reason or to the natural imagination (p. 35). The person of Christ is the peak of
supernaturality, according to Christian belief, because in
him the first and second causes are united as the center of
personal activity. This divine action exceeds the limits of
natural human experience and could not be understood
without revealed images through which persons are able to
think about and to apprehend something of this mystery.
The thought of Jesus was expressed in certain dominant
images, and the events of his life, death, and resurrection
provide an interpretation of these images and of the images
of the history of Israel.

> The great images interpreted the events of Christ's ministry,
> death and resurrection, and the events interpreted the images;
> the interplay of the two is revelation. Certainly the events with-
> out the images would be no revelation at all, and the images
> without the events would remain shadows on the clouds. (P. 43)

At times Farrer seems to be saying that the images are
occasions for the apprehension (pp. 35, 42). In contrast to
Finite and Infinite, however, the emphasis falls more strongly
on "occasion" than upon "apprehension." It is the mystery
that is set forth, and the apprehension is a description of the
mystery. There is no possibility of appealing behind the

image to a nonimaginative apprehension by which the image could be judged. The reality is given only through the images themselves.

Farrer adopts Gabriel Marcel's distinction between a problem, which allows of a solution, and a mystery, which can only be described. Rational theology, and metaphysics generally, deal with mysteries and not with problems. The function of analogy in rational theology is to describe the mystery of infinite being. Herein lies the basic shift in emphasis between the concepts of language and image in the earlier work and those employed in *The Glass of Vision*. The function of language is to describe the mystery rather than to indicate the apprehension. Description involves the use of multiple images, the formation of sentences, and the activity of discourse, whereas indicating or pointing does not. Description involves not only seeing, but also sketching, creating, and imagining.

> Since the human mind understands in the act of discourse, and not by simple intuition, to understand will be to describe. The metaphysician seeks to understand his mysteries in seeking to describe them. (P. 67)

The metaphysician selects certain analogies of common usefulness in order to construct a system that will be coherent and comprehensive, but his selection is from the images of free description. Free existential description is prior to metaphysics and provides the images that are ordered by the system.

> Metaphysics undertakes the whole complex of natural mysteries, free existential description takes them piecemeal, and the use the two methods make of analogy differs according to their aim and scope: but both use analogy, and in essentially the same way, that is, descriptively and critically. (P. 73)

The Christian theologian draws not only from the images of free description, but primarily from the revealed images of God's supernatural action.

From analogy with his knowledge of finite mysteries, the rational theologian suspects that his awareness of God arises out of his active relation to him. But he does not enter into relation with God as he does with other selves. The relation of creature to creator is a unique relation; God does not enter and leave the field of human activity. Creation is neither an action nor a passion of human existence. Knowledge of God must be mediated by finite substance, but it does not arise in a particular, determinate activity as does knowledge of others. How, then, does the mind come to discourse about the infinite? If divine activity is only a shadow that underlies all human activity equally, there seems to be no way for it to catch the attention of the human mind. If it creates no perturbations, or makes no difference in human experience, then there is no way for man to notice it in order to discourse about it.

> Our minds, in fact, are neither mirrors nor containers: their receptivity depends on what they can *do*, on their ability to busy themselves with their object, to express it in discoursing on it. But it seems that our minds are impotent to discourse on God, to express God. . . . Only in proportion as our experience of finite existence affords analogies in terms of which God can be discoursed upon, shall we be able, in discoursing on God, to actualize an apprehension of God; for without discourse there is no intellectual apprehension. (Pp. 86–87)

The mind involuntarily takes some aspect of finite existence as a shadow of the infinite, and this is the point of departure of rational theology. An act of discourse about the infinite is forced upon the mind by some experience of the finite. Perhaps it is the phenomenon of the freedom of the will, of the aspiration of the intellect, of the starry heavens above or the moral law within. In any of these cases the mind might find itself interpreting the finite phenomenon in terms of the infinite, and thus drawn into thought or discourse concerning the infinite. Discourse or thought, of course, involves language, hence language is an integral part of the experience.

This is a statement of the two-sided or correlative character of the act of knowing. We know the infinite only in correlation with our knowing of the finite. In *Finite and Infinite*, the apprehension of the infinite was said to be correlative with that of the finite, but the act of discourse was not present. Here Farrer says that there can be no intellectual apprehension without discourse. The correlation not only is a spatial one of several images simultaneously superimposed, but it also involves a temporal moment. The act of discourse about the infinite is also discourse about the finite and involves a clarification of and addition to self-knowledge. It is not only that one leaps from a prior knowledge of finite substance in the self to recognition of the infinite, but that the activity of discourse is also productive of further knowledge of the self.

The process of involuntary discourse about the infinite through the finite is viewed under the rubric of man's natural knowledge of God. This awareness of the infinite in the finite is natural to our human existence. It is a mystery of human nature. There is no way in which this mystery may be circumvented in order that man may apprehend God in some manner other than through the finite. God cannot even be named outside of this analogical awareness, because the awareness is tied to the experience of discourse and thus to the images and the analogies of which the discourse is composed. The rational theologian is not able to appeal to an apprehension beyond these analogies and images; he is able only to confront them with one another.

From his treatment of man's natural knowledge of God, Farrer moves to discuss the images of revelation. The correlative perception of the infinite through the finite in the social relations of human existence leads to the construction of certain human functions as types of divine archetypes. Thus in primitive communities, functions such as father, judge, and king are each understood to possess their power from a divine archetypal father, judge, or king. These archetypes arise simultaneously with their earthly counterparts.

The act of incarnation is a supernatural act, beyond the limits of human nature. If man is to know the divine action, images must be revealed to him by which he can know it. Jesus clothed himself in the archetypal images of Israel and acted, suffered, died and was raised, thus transforming the images (p. 109). The images are transformed and are made intelligible to faith by God's supernatural action. Faith discerns the act that the images signify, though it discerns this act only through the images. The criticized images that make up the analogies of natural theology may be used as a canon in terms of which to judge the revealed images, and within the revelation itself, the principal images provide a canon to the lesser ones (p. 111). This is not a matter of an immediate source of apprehension by which the images are accepted or rejected, but it is rather a confrontation of the images over against each other in discourse: the subordinate images against the principal images, and the revealed images against the criticized images of natural theology.

Farrer discusses the apprehension through images in the process of inspiration by a comparison of divine inspiration with that of the creative poet. Apprehension is not possible without an act of creative imagination. Inspiration is a process of living images imposing themselves with some kind of authority or constraint upon the thought of the inspired. In creative poetry the images cannot be separated from that which they symbolize, but this is not true of the prophets. The prophetic message has a certain definite content of information that may be expressed in more prosaic terms. Farrer suggests that poetry is a technique of divinization for the prophet.

The selection and interpretation of images in revelation is effected by the supernatural work of Christ and of the Holy Spirit. The original images are born and shaped in social and historical experience. They are part of the furniture of the natural world. They arise from human reflection on human experience, from man's attempt to describe his physical and political environment. The prophets and kings of Israel selected from these descriptive images and endowed some with certain interpretations of God's action and his plans for his people. The political and social history of Israel functioned in this selection by reinforcing some of the images and by exposing the inadequacy of others. The interplay of historical experience and prophetic interpretation was the revelation of God in the history of Israel, and this revelation prepared the images for the fulfillment of God's promise. Jesus took up these images and those of the Gentiles into his teaching and his action. His selection and interpretation by word and by act transformed the images into a revelation of the supernatural action of God in the incarnation of his son. The images were reborn; a new interpretation was provided for the old images and birth was given to new ones. This is the burden of the doctrine of the incarnation.

It is clear that Farrer's understanding of the role of image and language in the knowledge of God underwent a change in the period between the two works we have considered. The change in emphasis may best be described as a move from an understanding of the primary function of language as indication, pointing in the direction of an apprehension, to an understanding of this function as description, imaginative discourse concerning a mystery. The former is modeled after the presentation of an object directly to the sight and the instantaneous grasp or awareness of this object. The latter is a recognition of the function of discourse and imagination, and of the temporal dimension in the activity of knowing. Knowing involves the creation of multiple images and the selection of some and the rejection of others. It involves imaginative creation as well as apprehension.

Understanding occurs only in the act of discourse. Intellectual apprehension is not possible apart from imagination and discourse. In *Finite and Infinite* Farrer assigns creativity to the activity of the will and neglects its function in the intellect and in imagination. To the intellect is assigned the much more passive function of apprehension. His development of the correlative concepts of solicitation and response and of the notion of character, however, provide the pattern for a description of the activity of the intellect that acknowledges the place of imagination and discourse in knowing. Solicitation and response and the concentration of mnemic matter in the self both involve duration. They contrast with the instantaneous and immediate character of apprehension.

Farrer's subsequent treatment of philosophical issues is much more discursive than his earlier work, even to the extent of the adoption of the literary form of a dialogue for his Gifford Lectures.[37] In addition, he turned to the study of imagery and reflection on the interpretation of images in the New Testament. He retained the visual model of apprehension, now transformed into the idea of the mediating image. But he did not return to the consideration of a theory of language that would account for the creation and interpretation of images.

The need for a theory of interpretation that accounts for the employment of symbols and images in thinking and discourse leads us to the social type and the work of Royce. It was an attempt to describe the process of interpretation that led Royce to a reconstruction of the notion of the self and its relation to language and community. As Tillich's ontology was found to be deficient for an account of the integrity of the individual and the autonomy of the self, Farrer's epistemology seems deficient for an account of the social and temporal character of the analogies and images that he so deftly employs.

Each of the figures under consideration was an accomplished public speaker. Tillich and Farrer were both renowned preachers, though their sermonic styles differ greatly. All three delivered superbly crafted lectures. It is particularly interesting, then, to consider their respective accounts of the ways in which language, and especially religious language, functions. To readers in the last quarter of the twentieth century, Royce's language is apt to seem the least compelling. His images appear quaint, overly folksy, and possess little power to engage the contemporary imagination. Farrer's prose may occasionally appear forbiddingly formal or somewhat precious, but it is clear and powerful. Tillich's language is not always clear, but it has the power to persuade and to edify that is characteristic of some of the best existentialist writing. And yet it may be Royce, whose prose lacks the power to engage the modern sensibility, whose work is most helpful in providing an adequate theoretical account of the manner in which language functions and of the power of expression.

NOTES

1. Austin Farrer, *Finite and Infinite: A Philosophical Essay* (London: Dacre Press, 1943; 2d ed., 1959), p. 12.

2. Ibid., p. 14.

3. Martin Buber, *I and Thou*, trans. R. G. Smith (Edinburgh: T. & Clark, 1937).

4. This doctrine is classically expressed in Wittgenstein's *Tractatus*: "The world is the totality of facts, not of things." Ludwig Wittgenstein, *Tractatus Logico-Philosophicus* trans. C. K. Ogden and F. P. Ramsey (London: Routledge and Kegan Paul, Ltd., 1922), 1:1.

5. Karl Barth, *Church Dogmatics*, ed. G. W. Bromiley and T. F. Torrance (Edinburgh: T. & T. Clark, 1957), 2/2.

6. Ibid. (1960), 3/2.

7. R. M. Hare, *The Language of Morals* (London: Oxford University Press, 1952). Also Barth, *Church Dogmatics*, 2/2.

8. The classical and most influential statement of this position is Kant's: "Nothing in the world—indeed nothing even beyond the world—can possibly be conceived which could be called good without qualification except a good will." Immanuel Kant, *Foundations of the Metaphysics of Morals*, trans. L. W. Beck (New York: The Liberal Arts Press, 1959), p. 9.

9. Note Tillich's difficulty in responding systematically from his position to Hirsch's employment of his categories to justify the Third Reich. Tillich has no difficulty knowing exactly where he stands on the issue, but he has trouble finding resources in his system to make the necessary discriminations. Paul Tillich, "Die Theologie des Kairos und die gegenwärtige geistige Lage; Offener Brief an Emmanuel Hirsch," *Theologische Blätter* 13, no. 11 (1934): 305–28.

10. Farrer, *Finite and Infinite*, p. 103.

11. "Existentialism, in short, is the endeavor to understand man by cutting below the cleavage between subject and object which has bedeviled Western thought and science since shortly after the Renaissance." Rollo May, "The Origins and Significance of the Existential Movement in Psychology," in *Existence: A New Dimension in Psychiatry and Psychology*, ed. R. May, E. Angel, H. Ellenberger (New York: Basic Books, 1958), p. 11.

12. See Robert Neville, "Some Historical Problems about the Transcendence of God," *The Journal of Religion* 47 (1967): 1–9.

13. Farrer, *Finite and Infinite*, p. 169.
14. Austin Farrer, *The Glass of Vision* (London: Dacre Press, 1948).
15. In the preface to the second edition of *Finite and Infinite*, written in 1959, Farrer notes that he had spoken of a genuine apprehension, but had been unable to point to an act of apprehending anything that was other than an act of approving a description. It is necessary, and possible, he says, to investigate the grammar of our speech and thus of our activity as human beings. See "Preface to the Second Edition," pp. ix–x. A move from indication of apprehension to concern with discourse and imagery is recognized in these paragraphs, which constitute the only change from the text of the first edition.
16. Farrer, *Finite and Infinite*, pp. 293–94. For further comments concerning the parallels between will and intellect, see pp. 51–52, 287–97.
17. In his writing since *Finite and Infinite*, Farrer has turned attention to the functions of myths and images, particularly in study of New Testament documents. In *The Glass of Vision* he adumbrates a theory of the functioning of images. While some of Farrer's analysis in *Finite and Infinite* displays a sensitivity to imagistic thinking, the explicit discussion of language in that work focuses on analogy and the model of a structure that is not complicit with the apprehension toward which it points. See especially Austin Farrer, *The Rebirth of Images* (London: Dacre Press, 1949).
18. Farrer, *Finite and Infinite*, pp. 5–6.
19. Farrer here differs from Barth. Barth (*Church Dogmatics*, 2/1: 226) also claims that we are driven to the word *analogy* rather than to *parity* or *disparity*. But none of these words, he says, is actually more adequate than either of the others. Whatever this might mean, it is not the tack that Farrer takes.
20. Farrer, *Finite and Infinite*, p. 88.
21. "We do not naturally apply the name 'analogy' to this likeness which lies in nearness on a continuous scale, for it does not seem as though two simples can be analogous when considered by themselves. Analogy supposes complexity in the things compared." Ibid., p. 90.
22. "About that which is simply unique there can be no discourse; we can only repeat its name, and say that it is itself and not any of the others." Ibid., p. 23.
23. Farrer makes a similar distinction between supernatural and preternatural in *The Glass of Vision* (pp. 22–25). Since we know the upper limit of the activity of the intellect, we are able to detect the supernatural and to distinguish it from the weird phenomena that belong to the lower levels of our nature. He likens knowledge of the intellect to our knowledge of a cone, where the sight of the luminous apex provides knowledge of the shape and type of cone, even if the shadowy base is obscured from vision.
24. Farrer, *Finite and Infinite*, p. 170.
25. For discussion and some criticism of this use of the analogy of proportionality, see John Glasse, "Doing Theology Metaphysically: Austin Farrer," *Harvard Theological Review* 59 (1966): 340–41.
26. Farrer, *Finite and Infinite*, pp. 55ff.
27. This procedure is reminiscent of the comment of Wittgenstein in the final lines of his *Tractatus Logico-Philosophicus* (6:54):

> My propositions serve as elucidations in the following way: anyone who understands me eventually recognizes them as nonsensical, when he has used them—as steps—to climb beyond them. (He must, so to speak, throw away the ladder after he has climbed up it.) He must transcend these propositions, and then he will see the world aright.

Farrer would not hold that the propositions and analogies are nonsensical when the top of the ladder has been reached, but they have no real relation to the unique object that is apprehended. The parallel between Farrer's procedure in this section and that of Wittgenstein in the *Tractatus* is instructive. Both interpret language in a way that is individualistic. Both consider language to be a realm of manipulable tags that refer to apprehensibles or to facts in the real world. In their descriptions of language both ignore or minimize the complicity of the observer and speaker in the discovery of facts and the use of language, although in the actual execution of their work both men show more recognition of this complicity than their analyses would imply. The movement of Farrer's thought from *Finite and Infinite* to *The Glass of Vision* is similar to that of Wittgenstein from the *Tractatus* to the *Philosophical Investigations*.

28. Farrer, *Finite and Infinite*, p. 65.

29. Farrer's Gifford Lectures comprise a study of *The Freedom of the Will* (New York: Charles Scribner's Sons, 1958). In his last published work, *Faith and Speculation* (New York: New York University Press, 1967), he reemphasizes the voluntaristic core of theism and minimizes the formalism that was still present in *Finite and Infinite*.

30. *Faith and Speculation*, p. 122.

31. *Ibid.*, p. 123.

32. A movement in this direction can be detected in *The Glass of Vision*. There he talks less of analogy and apprehension and more of image and metaphor, which suggests that the metaphor remains to mediate the disclosure.

33. Farrer, *Finite and Infinite*, p. 114.

34. A similar appeal is contained in Dorothy Emmet's discussion of "adverbial" experience in contrast to the differentiated "accusative" experience of the particular senses. Dorothy Emmet, *The Nature of Metaphysical Thinking* (London: Macmillan and Company, 1945).

35. Farrer, *Finite and Infinite*, p. 265.

36. Farrer, *The Glass of Vision*, p. 8.

37. Austin Farrer, *The Freedom of the Will* (New York: Charles Scribner's Sons, 1958).

4

The Self in Community: The Social Type

The third typical conception to be considered is one in which the social or communal metaphor is fundamental. The later work of Josiah Royce will serve to illustrate this conception. Royce was concerned throughout his writing to elaborate a metaphysics that would account for both epistemological and ethical aspects of experience. From his earliest work in *The Religious Aspect of Philosophy* (1885), he attempted to set out a doctrine of the Absolute that was arrived at primarily through epistemological analysis. A metaphysical idealism was developed in order to account for the experience of error. At the same time his interest in eithics provided a strong voluntarism in his writings that was in some tension with his idealism. Royce did not want to lose the individual self as a center of will and activity in his attempt to sketch the Absolute. This led to a development throughout his writing in which the notion of the Absolute is interpreted as an ordered whole, a process, and finally as a society or community with a unifying purpose. A social and temporal character is gradually built into the basic idealist framework as Royce faces problems arising from the experience of human knowing, morality, and religion. This development comes to its fullest statements in *The Philosophy of Loyalty* (1908), The Bross Lectures on *The Sources of Religious Insight* (1912), and *The Problem of Christianity* (1913). Attention will be focused on the last of these works, since it contains the most extensive and complete treatment of Royce's mature metaphysical position.[1]

THE TYPE

The third type is a metaphysics of community. A person or self is described in social terms. Time is understood as pervasive of all of experienced reality and cannot be transcended in metaphysical description. The processes by which individuals differentiate themselves from and relate to other individuals in a social order are issues for metaphysics. Both individuals (selves) and wholes (communities) are studied in mutual correlation. It is impossible under this conception to begin, even theoretically, with isolated individuals or with undifferentiated wholes. Both of these notions are theoretically impossible as well as unfounded in our experience. Individuals are emergent within temporal and social processes.

Epistemology. The doctrine of signs and the concept of interpretation that Royce develops in *The Problem of Christianity* on the basis of certain insights gleaned from Peirce is a direct criticism of the epistemology of the second type. Royce argues that the knowing relation is not dyadic, but triadic. Another self or object is never encountered in immediate apprehension. Even my own inner self is not a datum of my experience. Language is not composed of tags that are assigned to objects of encounter or apprehension. Rather, language is the result of and the means for a continuing process of interpretation. Knowing always involves constructing an interpretation of a particular experience for a specific person. This is the case even if I am attempting to interpret something to myself and am engaged in the process of thinking.

Interpretation is a process. It takes time, unlike the experience of being grasped by a symbol or of encountering or being addressed by an other. Both of the latter images suggest momentary flashes of insight that may be preceded by preparation and followed by appropriation but that are immediate and atemporal events. Interpretation takes time and it is a social process. To say that interpretation is triadic rather than dyadic again sets it apart from immediate encounters with symbols or other selves. There is always a third, which mediates between two. An interpreter interprets a text or a fact to another person. I can interpret something to myself, but this relation cannot be reduced. The thing to be interpreted, the one to whom it is interpreted, and the third that mediates or interprets are all necessary to the relation. The social and temporal character of knowing is not ascribed to the limitations of finite existence and abstracted when we consider what ideal knowledge could be. This latter is the case, for instance, in Tillich's discussion of ecstasy and in Buber and Bultmann when they speak of interpersonal encounter. Rather, the temporality and sociality of knowing are the salient characteristics of the term that Royce employs to discuss the character of knowing. The doctrine that knowing is a process of interpretation has far-reaching consequences for the metaphysical position that results.

Language is social in character. My knowledge of myself is an interpretation constructed from my own experience and from my experience of others and of their interpretations of me. Knowledge does not begin with the hard datum of self-awareness and proceed by analogical jumps to other persons and objects. The learning process is social, and the self's awareness of itself becomes increasingly differentiated. A highly developed self-awareness is a rather sophisticated stage in the process.

This same point is made in Ludwig Wittgenstein's discussion of the impossibility of a private language.[2] The division of the world into individual atomic facts in his *Tractatus* stressed private intuition and the immediacy of the ostensive definition and of analogical knowledge. But Wittgenstein later became convinced that this view was false as an account of the functions of language, and in the *Philosophical Investigations* he stressed the social character of language. An individual comes to know himself through the words, the actions, and the subtle responses of others, and also by observing his own activity in certain situations. Wittgenstein notes that persons are often unable to predict their actions or even to declare their intentions unambiguously before they act. They just act. This is especially true of linguistic activity. The learning of a language is a social process in which one's conception of himself develops as he moves into different levels of activity and discourse. Each individual adds novelty to the language by his particular choice and new juxtapositions of words. The language to which he adds, however, is a public language and one in which he must respect the meanings and connotations of words. His novelty is woven on and into a social fabric. This fabric of the language depends upon a community of persons who are faithful to the language. It is this fidelity that provides the basis for the ability of the language to function in communication. Words are not arbitrary tags that are attached to objects of direct apprehension as those who attempt to derive language from ostensive definitions would have it. They are conventional signs that are constantly in the process of modification and reinterpretation.

In this third conception knowledge of God is not prior to all other knowledge as it is in the monistic type. Nor is self-knowledge the original touchstone, with knowledge of God reached only through a long chain of analogies that aid immediate apprehension, as in the individualistic type. Knowledge of self and knowledge of God are correlative. They develop with the initial differentiation of the self from its environment. Both appear and gradually become more determinate with the increasing differentiation of a social consciousness.

Ontology. In the ontology of the third type, social relations are considered as the paradigm for metaphysical relations. The world is understood as a community. Time is important for ontology. The ontological elements are not beyond time. The first two types involved constant striving to escape the temporal. This does not mean that Tillich and Farrer deny the experience of time, but rather that the metaphysical models that result from their analyses are abstractions from the time process that focus on the whole that underlies temporal change (Tillich) or on the moment of apprehension or decision that is caught in an instant like a snapshot (Farrer). Royce understands the time process and the phenomena of memory and expectation to be essential to an understanding of community. A cross-sectional view of experience may appear to produce a picture of the world as an aggregate of individuals, but if the common memories and expectations are observed and the language is studied, the complex network of relationships that make up any community will come into view. Interpretation, which is the paradigm not only for communication between these individuals but for the appropriation and integration of past and future with the present in any one individual, takes words and takes time. It is not instantaneous as is apprehension. It is discursive and mediate, as opposed to the immediacy of either the transparent symbol or the bare apprehension of dyadic encounter.

Royce pays more attention to the physical body and to the natural environment than do either the first or the second type. Common experiences and memories that involve interpretation embrace things as well as persons. Neither self-knowledge nor knowledge of things that we encounter in daily experience is available without interpretation. There is not the complete separation between knowledge of persons and knowledge of things that often is the case in the second type.[3] Hegel and Royce both understand the natural environment to be invested with value insofar as it is valued by human communities. Theirs is a social theory of value. The Hegelian Spirit or the Roycean Community attaches value to a particular event or locale through common memories and expectations. The event or locale then comes to have a value that makes a claim on that community and perhaps on others. The event of the Exodus and the state of Israel are examples of an event and a locale that have been given value through common experience and that now contain that value in themselves so that association with this event and this state can appear to bestow values on others.

Royce portrays God as identical with the Kingdom of Heaven or the Community of Interpretation. God is social. He is the idealization of communities of memory and hope in which individuals find themselves. This idealization is not abstract or unrelated to specific communities. Rather, the conception of the ideal involves the extrapolation and extension of specific concrete communities of human history. This notion of the infinite community is parallel to Hegel's discussion of the concrete Absolute or to Royce's own struggle with the notion of an actual infinite. It is not opposed to the particular and the concrete, but is an extension or extrapolation of the concrete.

God is the infinite community of interpretation in which each individual is comprehended and in which all relations are harmonious. This community is a network of perfect social harmony. God is identified with the coming of his rule, or with his Kingdom. Temporality is characteristic of God as it is of the world. God is not beyond space and time, but is the fulfillment of both. The continuity of the being of God with social and natural experience is stressed. God's transcendence is expressed not in terms of radical discontinuity and otherness, or in terms of transcendental conditions, but by the appeal to his comprehensiveness and to the character of his governing of the world process.

Ethics. The social character of the human situation is both the cause of man's sin and the key to his transformation or redemption. Estrangement or sin in a world interpreted as community is disruption, lack of communication, opacity, and isolation. In his description of the moral burden of the individual, Royce identifies Paul's divided self with the tension between the individual competitive will and the need and desire for communal cooperation. Both the autonomous individual with his own ego and centered self and the corporate citizen who recognizes his interdependence with his fellows are products of the socialization process. As this process develops, both of these aspects are strengthened and the burden of the tension is exacerbated. Thus the division in man that Royce identifies as the moral burden of the individual is a source of continual and increasing conflict. This is the reality described by the Christian doctrine of sin.

This interpretation of sin as the fact of the anxiety or tension within the individual, between his own egocentric interests with their tendency to make himself the center of the world, and his sense of himself as a communal or social being, provides a framework in which the descriptive truth of the traditional doctrine of sin can be interpreted in the light of new understanding of the relationship of the individual psyche to society. Knowledge of the processes of projection, internalization, the trying-on of various role models, developing one's identity by differentiating oneself from his family or from persons who threaten his own sense of autonomy, and the appropriation of new roles and relations in the search for identity can all aid in the interpretation of what was earlier discussed as sin and redemption. Tillich's discussion of sin as estrangement is fruitful in its ability to illumine and to draw upon the insights of depth psychology. But the description of sin and anxiety as estrangement has generally been discussed within the context of a psychology in which the emphasis is upon the individual. The individual is either considered in his estrangement from himself (the isolated view of man in existentialism) or from being, or in his estrangement from the ground of that being, which is interpreted as some mystical unity (Jung). In either case the development of an interpretation of estrangement or anxiety in relation to the immediate social processes in which an individual is immersed and the differentiation of the individual from his fellows is either ignored or preempted. The differences between persons and other aspects of nature are not rendered intelligible but are ascribed to basic metaphysical or mystical differences. Why should the estrangement of a self from the ground of its being produce existential *Angst* and sin while the estrangement of a stone from its ground is relatively minor? The answer implicit in the existential approach is that there is all the difference in the world, nay more, between persons and stones. What is this difference? Persons have wills, can decide, act, exist! Stones only are. This is hardly an intelligible explanation, and it serves only to raise the distinction between persons and stones (or dolphins) into a cosmic distinction. The interpretation of sin in terms of the inauthenticity of decision within the individualistic type also elevates the distinction between persons who have will and others who do not into a cosmic distinction. Royce understands will and the process of choice to be involved in the moral burden of the individual, but he interprets the development of this will and the process by which this tension occurs in terms that are intelligible in the light of our understanding of biological and psychosocial processes. An individual will is not a happy possession of some entities and not of others. It develops within a social context as an infant grows into a mature person, and as the human race develops from primitive to more complex stages of existence.

Loyalty is Royce's central ethical term. Royce's voluntarism is explicit in his later work. Harmony in voluntaristic terms is loyalty. Loyalty to the infinite or beloved community is love for God and is parallel to Tillich's concern for being-itself. The paradigm of sin is betrayal or disloyalty. Betrayal is not only idolatry, which may be naive, nor is it defiance or disobedience as in the second type. It is also the betrayal of an ego-centered individual who has known real love and community with his fellows and who betrays that community. The self is divided because he has betrayed the community that is part of his own being. It is false love, or the willful sabotage of what one knew to be good. It is not just a conflict of wills but a betrayal of social value, which the traitor himself acknowledges. It is the betrayal of a friend. Judas is the paradigmatic sinner.

Royce's doctrine of atonement differs from both of the previous types in that it involves not only restoration, but the production of a new community and of harmonies that were previously impossible. Value and meaning are constantly produced and expanded. The end of God's activity is not restoration but sanctification and the bringing to birth of a new community. Atonement is the use of an occasion provided by sin to bring about an increase in being and value that otherwise could not have occurred. The time process is crucial. God's love creates a new community even out of man's sinful relationships. Again Royce's interpretation is rooted in a description of social processes. The traitor who has betrayed not only another but an aspect of the values that he holds dearest cannot be reconciled merely by expressing regret and having a parent or a civil judge or some other figure of authority forgive him in the manner of a forensic decision. This pattern is suitable for a child who has done something wrong in the eyes of his parents. The proscription of the act came from the parents and the decision to forgive and forget can also come from them. This is the model that informs the interpretation of divine justice as forensic decision that is prominent in the individualistic Lutheran doctrine of justification and the righteousness of God.

It is also impossible for the traitor to be reconciled by losing himself and merging into the community again. The proscription of his act and the guilt are his and are not externally imposed upon him. The only way in which some reconciliation can be achieved is for him to relate to his fellows and also to himself as someone who was indeed the author of this deed and who seeks a new kind of basis for the community between them. Lost innocence is not recoverable. Husband and wife, parent and child, friend and partner must all go on from each event that presents itself to work out a new relationship that comprehends that event, even if it was an event that involved betrayal, and that builds a new understanding. It is illusory and disastrous if they attempt to recover a relationship that existed in the past and to take refuge in that. Time cannot be stopped and reconciliation involves building communication and trust with full recognition of what has happened. It is often the case that the new relationship is firmer and the trust is deeper after some of these incidents than it had been previously. Spouses who have been through conflict as well as joyous experiences share mutual knowledge and trust that is not to be found in two persons whose time together has been pleasant but short and relatively superficial. It is this process of the development of depth in personal and social relationships to which Royce refers when he speaks of bringing new being and value out of conflict and betrayal. It is not some optimistic vision of good coming out of everything, which might be worthy of a Polyanna.

Being is not an eternal state from which one is estranged and in which one participates in moments of ecstasy or periods of theonomy. There is no fixed amount of value in the world that must be distributed and redistributed in the face of poverty and inequality. God's loving activity and human creativity are constantly productive of increase in interpretation, value, and being. This increase is the building of the Beloved Community.

THE ONE AND THE MANY

The analysis of Tillich as a representative of the monistic type began with his distinction between the ontological and cosmological approaches to religion and his stated preference for the ontological. The ontological approach involves a unity and an immediacy that he felt could never be recovered if one began with the pluralistic view of the universe characteristic of the cosmological method. At the outset of the chapter on the individualistic type it was noted that Farrer also contrasted these two approaches and judged that the cosmological approach, starting from a plurality of entities, was the only legitimate one. Any form of the ontological argument that actually illumines the relation of finite and infinite must be grounded in a disguised form of the cosmological method. Similarly, Tillich had said that the cosmological method can prove effective if it functions as a hidden employment of the ontological approach.

The significance of beginning with each of these contrasts is to note the fact that all of the figures under study were aware and self-conscious of the major metaphysical options that are here being compared and contrasted and of some of their relative merits and limitations. Their choice of one perspective was made in the light of this awareness. This awareness strengthens the case for the integrity and viability of each of these options and minimizes the possibility of treating any of these positions as straw men. The type of analysis that involves the erection of a new set of categories, purported to be on a higher level of generality than the work being considered, can often be illuminating, but it runs serious risks. By moving to another level it transcends and thus preempts, at the beginning of the analysis, the arguments that have been given in the work under consideration. Some of this risk is undoubtedly present in the consideration of the three types in this study. The risk is lessened, however, by the fact that each of the figures recognized the issues and some of the alternative modes of proceeding. The present analysis is not a case of bringing some novel framework that was unconsidered by each of the authors and chastising them for not taking that framework into account. An aim of this study is to evaluate the several conceptions and to suggest a framework in which articulations of the relationship between finite and infinite that arise out of various aspects of individual and communal experience can be comprehended and integrated. But the questions are posed on a level that, for the most part, was recognized by each of the authors under discussion.

It is fitting then to begin the discussion of Royce with a passage in which he also recognizes and contrasts the alternative of monistic and pluralistic metaphysical approaches, and in which he sketches his own procedure.

> The altogether too abstractly stated contrast between Monism and Pluralism—a contrast which fills so large a place in the metaphysical writings of the day, does not force itself to the front, in our minds and in our words, when we set out to inquire into the real basis of the idea of the community. For a community immediately presents itself to our minds both as one and as many; and unless it is both one and many, it is no community at all. This does not, by itself, solve the problem of the One and the Many. But it serves to remind us how untrue to life is the way in which that problem is frequently stated.
> In fact, as I believe, the idea of the community, suggested to us by the problem of human social life, but easily capable of a generalization which possesses universal importance, gives us one of our very best indications of the way in which the problem of the One and the Many is to be solved, and of the level of mental life upon which the solution is actually accomplished.[4]

Royce is proposing the notion of community as one that comprehends both the one and the many and provides a coherent account of both of these aspects of human experience. It might be suggested that every thinker attempts something similar. He tries to show that his own account comprehends all other possibilities. This is indeed the case, but the extrapolation to the comprehensive view proceeds in different ways. There is a discontinuity between the descriptions of the state of finitude offered by both Tillich and Farrer and their ideal descriptions of the infinite or of God. This can be illustrated in Tillich by recalling the distinction between the conditions of existence that is characterized by polarities, and the being of God, in which all of the polarities are transcended or overcome. Thus fullness of being can be tasted occasionally in moments of ecstatic awareness that lift us out of our ordinary existence and that therefore appear as discontinuous with finite nature, though they help to illumine that nature. Similarly, Farrer employs a dialectical analysis throughout *Finite and Infinite,* and especially in the arguments that are the culmination of the work, the main purpose of which is to enable the reader to jump from his oscillation in the dialectical description of human experience to an apprehension of something beyond, other than, and discontinuous with that experience. Both Tillich and Farrer make use of dialectic to aid in the bridging of this discontinuity. Conditions such as those of temporality and sociality can be left behind in the dialectical jump to the infinite, because these are conditions that characterize finite existence but that are transcended in an analysis of the infinite.

Royce was a self-proclaimed idealist in his metaphysics and is often portrayed as someone who escapes quickly from the specific experience of mundane life to the abstractions of idealism. This is not the case. Royce's thought underwent considerable development from *The Religious Aspect of Philosophy* (1885) through *The World and The Individual* (1899, 1901) to *The Problem of Christianity* (1913). This development involved an increasing emphasis upon the world conceived as a community of individual selves in time as opposed to his earlier conceptions of the Absolute, which insufficiently stressed both the temporal character of existence and individuality. But even in his earlier discussions of logic and mathematics and his formulation of the Absolute, Royce was concerned to develop an adequate account of the concrete infinite.[5] He was and remained committed to the notion of a unity, an absolute, or a community that he held was given in human experience of thinking and of morality as well as religion. But the articulation of this unity must retain the concreteness of the specific experiences in which it is given. It would be inadequate for a philosopher or for a philosophical theologian to invoke dialectic or the character of God as "wholly other" in order to escape the task of accounting for some aspects of experience.

Every metaphysician extrapolates from common experience to abstractions or conceptions that he feels are more universal and illuminating than are other possible abstractions. It is significant to note what aspects of experience are chosen as the basis for the extrapolation. This is especially significant in the philosophy of religion. In dealing with religion it is tempting to take as examples of religious experience certain states of consciousness that are esoteric or uncharacteristic of ordinary experience. Tillich attempted to avoid this pitfall and to root his descriptions of religion in common notions such as "concern" and experiences of doubt and anxiety. In spite of his brilliance in relating the symbols and doctrines of Christian theology to the experience of individuals and of cultures, his model for the ideal religious experience is that of the mystic, of the moment of ecstasy and union with the ground of being. When he describes the experience of being grasped by a symbol, the criticism of parochial concerns by the ultimate, or existential anxiety in the face of contemporary meaninglessness, he identifies each of these as manifestations of an experience that comes from behind, that is rare, and that is enjoyed or tasted most fully by those who are sensitive to the monistic vision.

Farrer does not hold up this experience of the mystic as the criterion for what in experience is to be called religious. His analysis in *Finite and Infinite* is grounded in a careful description of human knowing and willing. But the notion of apprehension to which the book is directed, the vision of God that may be attained if one directs his attention and can grasp the *Gestalt* of the finite-infinite relation, is also based on the tradition of the *visio dei* as the highest achievement of human life and knowledge that is granted finally to the saints. Farrer entitles his lectures on the inspiration of biblical authors and of the saints of the Church *The Glass of Vision*, reflecting again the tradition of the *visio dei*.

Both of these approaches judge the religious aspect of human experience in the light of an ideal immediate experience of God that is attributed finally to the saint. Royce, on the other hand, interprets as religious the common experiences of daily life. He seldom refers to a conception of the saint, though one can infer that a saint in his community would be one who did not stand out in isolation as having experienced a mystical unity with the absolute or a vision of God but one who was most active in the community, who recognized and enjoyed his dependence upon his fellows in the community as well as his own ability to provide resources for personal strength and knowledge to others who might be in need. The experience on which he drew was that of colleagues and students within the university community.[6] His ideal was not the saint who was set apart, but the member of the social fabric. This becomes clear in his contention that the Christian Church stems not from Jesus or an individual founder, but from the community of Christians who came together to try to interpret the meaning of their experience or of the reports that they had heard concerning the life and death of Jesus.

Another way of expressing the comprehensive character of Royce's notion of the community and of the process of interpretation in addressing the problem of the one and the many is the combination of both voluntarism and idealism in his thought. He was concerned to account for the individuation of persons, which is most evident in their deeds and in the notion of will. This was combined with a conviction that a critique of human knowing as well as an analysis of the values involved in moral choice both led to the affirmation of an ideal that unites all knowing and all valuing. But this ideal could not be merely a construction of the intellect or of the imagination. It must also be related to the activity of the will. Hence the words that are prominent in Royce's idealism are words that are connected with action. Loyalty and interpretation within community involve acts of devotion, occasional betrayal, and the constant forging of new relations within a community. Fidelity and betrayal as well as novel relationships are also applicable to the use of language and signs and the process of interpretation. Royce's voluntarism was a point of contract between his thought and that of William James and the philosophy of pragmatism. But Royce was never satisfied with a functional account of the role of religion or of the role of language in human experience. That functional account was essential for him, but it was also necessary for the philosopher to go on and to attempt to provide an integrated and coherent account of the unity of experience. This involved raising the question of the truth of a scientific hypothesis or a religious doctrine as well as investigating its function.

THE SELF IS NOT A DATUM

Royce is explicit in *The Problem of Christianity* in stating his debt to some of the early papers of Charles Sanders Peirce for key conceptions in his metaphysics.[7] He is also quick to note that he has extended the use of these concepts beyond the point of Peirce's employment of them and probably beyond what Peirce would have sanctioned. The theory of interpretation as a mode of cognition, the doctrine of signs, the conception of a community of interpretation, and the denial of an intuitive self-consciousness are all ideas that come directly from Peirce's work. The denial of an intuitive self-consciousness is argued in a short section of one of Peirce's early papers.[8] This argument had a strong influence on Royce and is extremely important for our consideration. It is a direct critique of the idea of the touchstone of knowledge, which underlies the epistemology of the individualistic type.

It was noted above that the epistemological approach characteristic of the second type begins with the conviction that a person possesses a priviliged access to his own self and thus has a knowledge of that self that is primary and is more immediate than any other object of knowledge. This is classically stated by Descartes when he discovers that he is able to doubt everything except his own existence as a doubting being: "I think therefore I am." From this last kernel of knowledge, the knowledge of his own ego, he slowly rebuilds the world, which had earlier fallen before his onslaught of doubt. *Touchstone* is the correct word for the Cartesian ego. Without it there would be no rock, no foundation on which to build. It is expressed also by Farrer, though in not quite so extreme a fashion. Farrer sets out to describe substance and decides that the only place where direct access to substance is possible is with the self as agent.

> I told myself that I had to reconstruct the doctrine of substance; by which I meant, that I could not be content to derive the structure of being from the grammar of description; I must unearth it where it could be genuinely apprehended. And where was that? Initially, anywhere, in myself, self-disclosed as the subject of my acts.[9]

This view is not only characteristic of the individualistic type. It is also a notion that appears to be supported by common sense, at least in the modern period of European and American culture. The autonomy of the individual that has developed in political, intellectual, and psychological terms in the West is built on a conception that each individual knows himself and his own desires best and in a way that is independent of what others think of him. The theory of the social contract upon which most democratic political theory rests treats each individual as the authority on his own needs and wants. When Freud and others demonstrate that some men are not really conscious of what they themselves need or desire but are tailoring their actions in response to other persons' images of them, it is taken for granted that these men are crippled and have been unable to develop into autonomous beings. This evidence of persons who easily forfeit their autonomy is often subtly used to make a far different point. That point is that every autonomous human being has privileged access to his own self that is unavailable to every one else and on analogy with which he projects his knowledge of others.

The notion of an intuitive self-consciousness had been criticized brilliantly by Kant in his "Refutation of Idealism" in the first critique.[10] But in spite of the title of the section, that argument had been carried out within the confines of Kant's own version of idealism. Royce, who had educated himself within the tradition of German idealism and felt that to be his real heritage, was often impressed by the arguments of Peirce because they were so empirically based. They took their departure from actual examples of common experience carefully observed, from the history of scientific thought, or from careful logical analysis. Their author was hailed as the genius behind pragmatism, whose commitment was to empiricism and common sense. Yet more than once these arguments confirmed notions that were congenial to Royce's own idealism. To have supporting or confirming arguments from a logician and scientist who was immune from the heady and cloudy conceptions of German idealism was especially heartening.[11] Royce was particularly impressed then by Peirce's argument against the possibility of an intuitive self-consciousness.[12]

Peirce's argument is very compact and takes its departure from observation of young children.[13] He begins by noting that young children seldom use the word *I*, although it is a common word. It takes time for this to develop. They develop other very sophisticated patterns of thought before they use the word *I*. They master the trigonometry of vision, and coordinate difficult movements, so that this cannot be accounted for by an inability to think at all. Children observe their bodies very closely. When they hear a bell they think of the ringing as in the bell. They don't first think "I have an impression of ringing in myself" and then argue out from that to the existence of a bell. Royce adds that some of this primitive experience can be observed in adults in moments of passion. When a man feels angry at another, his primary feeling is not "I am angry" and then "That man is the object of my anger." Rather, his first sensation is that the object of his anger is despicable and blameworthy. Only upon reflection does he realize "I am angry." The self-knowledge of his own state is not primitive, followed by attention to something that must be the object of that emotion or sensation. Rather, the sensation is felt to be in the object, and it is only by responding to the object and observing one's own response that a person comes to an awareness of his own emotional state.[14]

This awareness involves time and interpretation. A person defines himself with relation to his own past and expectations for the future. Much of his understanding of himself comes from other persons and their responses toward him. Peirce points out that this dependence upon the perceptions and testimony of others is not confined to children. Testimony of the community can convince an adult that he is mad. Anthropologists cite cases in which communal testimony or the magical words of the shaman supported by the community can cause a person to lie down and die "against his own will." That is to say, the power of combined testimony can kill him.[15] An individual's image of himself is formed by interpreting his own experience as well as his experience of others responding to him. The development of the ability to speak and to use more sophisticated linguistic constructions parallels the development of the psyche in the child, as Piaget and others have shown. This language contains within it the fabric of the community or society for which it provides the means of communication. Language is not only convention, but is convention supported by the fidelity of a community. It is this support that gives power to the magic of the shaman in a primitive tribe. It is also this support that provides the context in which a child develops his own sense of. himself as differentiated first from his mother, then from his father and other members of his environment. There is much more data from the study of child psychology available today than there was at the time at which Royce wrote and it confirms and states in much more sophisticated terminology the basic point that he made: Knowledge of the self is not independent of the community in which that self develops. Descartes was wrong in supposing that the *cogito* is the foundation of all knowing.

Knowledge of the self is dependent upon social intercourse and upon the responses of others. Knowledge of the self also takes time. The *cogito* as Descartes described it was an intuition. Farrer spoke of unearthing an apprehension of the self. Tillich also speaks of an immediate intuition of the self either in moments of anxiety or moments of ecstasy. These function as moments of self-disclosure when the particular state in which one finds oneself becomes completely transparent to the ground of its being and the self is disclosed without mediation. It is the supposition that this immediate knowledge of self-disclosure is possible and is the ideal by which we judge all other knowledge that is denied by Peirce and Royce. Knowledge of the self, like all other knowledge, is always mediated. It must be interpreted. Interpretation takes time, and it has a social character.

> These facts about our individual self-consciousness [illustrations that Royce has presented] are indeed well known. But they remind us that our idea of the individual self is no mere present datum, or collection of data, but is based upon an interpretation of the sense, of the tendency, of the coherence, and of the value of a life to which belongs the memory of its own past.[16]

> This power [the power of an individual to extend himself ideally in time through memory and hope] itself rests upon the principle that, however a man may come by his idea of himself, the self is no mere datum, but is in its essence a life which is interpreted, and which interprets itself, and which, apart from some sort of ideal interpretation, is a mere flight of ideas, or a meaningless flow of feelings, or a vision that sees nothing, or else a barren abstract conception. How deep the process of interpretation goes in determining the real nature of the self, we shall only later be able to estimate. (2:61)

Royce portrays self-knowledge as discursive in the way in

which a community of selves would arrive at common knowledge by mutual contribution and criticism. He begins this discussion by considering a scientific community and the way in which results of the researches and hypotheses of individuals become appropriated by the community. An individual frames a hypothesis, designs an experiment to test that hypothesis, conducts the experiment, and then attempts to interpret the results. But his hypothesis, the design and control of his experiment, and his interpretation of the results of that experiment all must be subjected to public scrutiny and criticism by his colleagues within the scientific community before they are accepted. Royce quotes a colleague of his from the natural sciences to the effect that public scrutiny among colleagues removes the personal idiosyncratic element from the theories or interpretations of an individual and allows them to be appropriated into the body of knowledge of the specific science. Royce does not agree that the personal character of the work is removed, but rather, it is criticized and corrected and appropriated by a community of peers. He takes this process of criticism and interpretation to be a paradigm of all knowing, even that knowing of oneself, which appears to take place in isolation.

There is no immediate knowledge that is not interpreted. Interpretation involves comparison and judgment. This comparison and judgment takes place within a community of persons and it takes place in time. The self is also described as a community by Royce. Self-knowledge occurs by the comparison between a self's present perceptions, its memories of the past, and its expectations for the future. I know myself now by means of comparison with my past experiences. Kant also had this insight but it was never clearly developed. The social and temporal character of existence receives no prominence in Kant's analysis, though it is implied by his notion of comparison and judgment. He implies that knowledge arises from judgment made on comparing past and present intuitions.

The self is described as a community or as a *polis*. In this broad sense Royce's interpretation of self and community is political. Conflict and the development of new relationships, of a new form of community, of a new self-image, are always occurring. Every judgment and interpretation must be reinterpreted. Past and future are constantly reevaluated and reappropriated.

> A community, like an individual self, must learn to keep the consciousness of its unity through the vicissitudes of an endlessly shifting and often dreary future. (2:81)

Royce's conception of the self is an instance of his conception of community. The comparison and judgment of different intuitions from the past and the present within the experience of one person recapitulate the comparison and judgment that occur in conversation and interpretation in any community.

Royce argues that time is necessary to community. In the language that has become fashionable in the decades since Royce spoke and wrote, it could be said that a community must have a history. Crowds or mobs, which often have common minds and can be manipulated or described in terms of mob psychology, are not communities. They are aggregates of individuals who are thrown together. Crowds have short memories, as gossip is short-lived. But a community is a group of persons who share a common history and common hopes. The obvious example is the community of Israel and the rehearsal in ritual form of the events of Israel's past.[17] Royce uses the example of New Zealand communities that trace their past back to a common canoe in which their ancestors traveled. In form, this is equivalent to the common event of the exodus in the history of Israel. A community looks not only backward, but also forward. It involves hope and expectation as well as memory. By ideally extending itself in the past (to a common canoe or exodus) or in the future (to the notion of a general resurrection) a community interprets itself. Again the analogy with the individual self is maintained.

> The rule that time is needed for the formation of a conscious community is a rule which finds its extremely familiar analogy within the life of every individual human self. Each of us knows that he just now, at this instant, cannot find more than a mere fragment of himself present. The self comes down to us from its own past. It needs and has a history. Each of us can see that his own idea of himself as this person is inseparably bound up with his view of his own former life, of the plans that he formed, of the fortunes that fashioned him, and of the accomplishments which in turn he has fashioned for himself. A self is, by its very essence, a being with a past.[18]

Royce cites three conditions that must be met in order to have community. The first is that there must exist the power of individual selves to extend their lives in ideal fashion into the past and the future. This is the power of ideally extending memory and hope. Such power might be attributed to the imagination, though Royce does not use that term. The second condition is that there are in the social world a number of distinct selves that are capable of communication and that do communicate. This is an important element, because it is a clear statement of the fact that the notion of community is not used by Royce as a ruse to introduce a conception of the Absolute that dissolves all individuality and recognizes only the whole. Community is made up of distinct individuals who communicate. The third condition is that the ideally extended pasts and futures of the selves who compose the members of a community have at least some events that are identical for all of the selves. Something such as the Exodus, the New Zealand canoe, the expectation of a second coming of Christ must provide a common event for the consciousness of those who are to make up a community.

A community must also be related to purpose or action. Community involves cooperation as well as understanding and love. Royce recognizes that cooperation alone does not make a community. Rather, this cooperation must be accompanied by a sense of common history and purpose.

> In fact, it is the original sin of any highly developed civilization that it breeds cooperation at the expense of a loss of interest in the community. . . .
> Men do not form a community, in our present restricted sense of that word, merely in so far as the men cooperate. They form a community, in our present limited sense, when they not only cooperate, but accompany that cooperation with that ideal extension of the lives of individuals whereby each cooperating member says: "This activity which we perform together, this work of ours, its past, its future, its sequence, its order, its sense,—all these enter into my life, and are the life of my self writ large." (2:85–86)

A community so conceived and so dedicated creates its own solution to the problem of the one and the many. The diversity of the members and the unity of the body in respect to the identical event in memory or hope are both essential aspects of the community. The description of the community and its extension to a description of the self comprehend both the one and the many.

INTERPRETATION AS A MODE OF COGNITION

Royce contrasts perception and conception and theories of knowledge that stress one or the other. Plato and Bergson serve as representatives of these two views. Plato understood all sense experience or perception to be the occasion by which we came to grasp concepts or the ideas of reality. These ideas were already present in our mind, but had been forgotten or obscured. Thus perception provided a catalyst or an occasion for increasing conceptual knowledge. Bergson proposed a primitivism or a return to the natural naive state of naked unadulterated perception. In a way analogous to Jean-Jacques Rousseau's essays on "progress" in human civilization, Bergson criticized contemporary European philosophy as having lost touch with the immediate perceptions of concrete experience. The instance of this view that Bergson treated most thoroughly was the contrast between measured scientific time and the raw experience of time or duration. This contrast was not unlike that suggested in recent decades by the contrast between *existential* analysis and *existentiell* analysis, the former of which is a detached analysis of the structures of existence and the latter a description of those structures as experienced from within the situation. It is also similar to Tillich's distinction between technical and ontological reason. These distinctions do not quite parallel the distinction between objective and subjective (although those connotations are present), but they suggest a contrast between direct intuition or raw experience and that experience which has been filtered through conceptual and cultural frameworks.

Kant had shown earlier and Royce reaffirms, on somewhat different grounds, that no such raw perceptual experience is possible. Nor is conception possible apart from relation to perceptual experience. There must be some third mode of cognition. It is in Peirce's discussion of knowing as interpretation that Royce finds this third mode. He has already shown that interpretation is involved in communal knowledge and even in self knowledge. Neither intuition nor conception will suffice.

> For the rest, nobody's self is either a mere datum or an abstract conception. A self is a life whose unity and connectedness depend upon some sort of interpretation of plans, of memories, of hopes, and of deeds. (2:111)

But the accounts of human knowing that are proposed by both Plato and Bergson are neither conceptions nor intuitions. They are both interpretations of the process of knowing. Interpretation, says Royce after Peirce, is a model that accounts for knowing as a process that takes time and that involves comparison and judgment.

The object of a perception is a datum or a thing. The object of a conception is some universal or quality. Does this exhaust all objects of cognition, asks Royce? If so, in which of these classes would you put your neighbor's mind? Or any of the acts of that mind? Or your own mind? None of these are directly intuited, nor are they conceived without any relation to experience. They are objects of interpretation.

Royce illustrates the relation of interpretation to perception and conception in several ways. He employs James's distinction between "cash-value" and "credit-value" and argues that something must mediate between credit (conception) and the cash (perception). That mediation is performed by the promise that provides backing for the credit and assurance that it can be redeemed for cash. He also uses the example of an exchange of currency at a boundary between two countries. Rubles are useless in Finland but can be exchanged (under ordinary conditions of some sort of community between Russia and Finland) at the border into Finnish currency. This process of exchange is a process of interpretation. The value of one currency is interpreted in terms of another.[19] Similarly, the interpretation of a message from one language to another demands an interpreter who mediates between Finnish and Russian.

Interpretation involves a triadic relation. This is extremely important. Royce is somewhat apologetic to the audience gathered for his lectures for his treatment of an issue of human experience in terms of such seemingly formal categories as dyadic and triadic. But, he says, this distinction can be that between poverty and wealth in a relationship. Interpretation always involves a relation between three things. There is an object or mind that is to be interpreted, the person to whom the interpretation is directed, and the interpreter or mediator.

Interpretation always involves a relation of three terms. In the technical phrase, interpretation *is* a triadic relation. That is, you cannot express any complete process of interpreting by merely

naming two terms,—persons or other objects,—and by then
telling what dyadic relation exists between one of these two and
the other. (2:140)

The model is taken from the situation of a linguistic interpretation. The Finn and the Russian engage someone
who understands both Finnish and Russian. But its application is much broader.

Knowledge never involves only naked intuition. That
which is presented to the senses is interpreted in terms of
previous experiences and conceptions of the percipient.
Through the present experience of the self, the past self is
interpreted to the future self. It is always a triadic relation.
Interpretation is also always an asymmetric relation. One
person interprets something to another. In that moment
the two individuals are involved in different roles, one as
interpreter and the other as he who receives the interpretation. It was noted above that the I-thou model of interpersonal encounter or of the meeting between two wills that
informs the epistemology and the ethics of the individualistic type is a symmetric relation. It is a relation of two confronting wills. This relation was likened to the point in the
development of the child in which the child discovers himself to be autonomous, to be a person or a self in interaction
with other selves. This is to be distinguished from the image
that informs the monistic type, which is that of the relation
of infant to mother, or the part in relation to the whole.
This paradigmatic relation of the social type is not dyadic as
is the individualistic relation. It is triadic and asymmetric. It
can be correlated with the experiences in the life cycle in
which the child or young adult moves beyond the need to
prove his own autonomy, to establish himself as an individual over against authorities as well as peers, and is able to
accept himself as a social being. He is autonomous, he understands himself to be an independent ego, and he does
not need continually to prove this independence to himself
and others by denying the interdependence of members in

the community of which he is a part. In childhood this experience begins when children begin to play with each other, to share toys, to negotiate disputes over possession and rules of games. In Freud's analysis of the stages of sexual growth, this experience comes with genitality and with the experience of intercourse, which also involves cooperation, mutual sensitivity, and negotiation of individual desires and needs for the sake of a common goal. It is not symmetric as in the ideal I-thou situation portrayed in the second type. Such a situation sometimes serves as a model for the fantasies of romantic love. Two persons who are "made for each other" discover one another and have a beautiful symmetric relationship with no need to negotiate, no conflicts. This fantasy often takes the form of a relationship in which no words need be spoken. This is significant, since words are the media of interpretation and negotiation. The verbal or interpretive relationship is asymmetric. The recent popularity of encounter groups (note that *encounter* is the ideal word of the second type) and nonverbal experience provides an example of the acting out of these fantasies of an immediate and symmetric relationship.

Royce realized that this idealization was not true to the processes of interpretation and negotiation that go on not only between persons but also within the self. These processes demand continual mediation, comparison, judgment, and reinterpretation. Interpretation is a conversation. It is a temporal enterprise and it is a social one. The process is continual. The temporal order involves the interpretation of the past to the future.

> The relations exemplified by the man who, at a given present moment, interprets his own past to his own future, are precisely analogous to the relations which exist when any past state of the world is, at any present moment, so linked, through a definite historical process, with the coming state of the world, that an intelligent observer who happened to be in possession of the facts could, were he present, interpret to a possible future the meaning of the past. (2:144–45)

This image of an ideal observer foreshadows Royce's discussion of the community of interpretation and of the unity that provides.

Interpretation is mediated, while both perception and conception seek for a knowledge that is immediate. They both seek to derive knowledge from something external to the self. Truth comes by revelation, or by remembering or being grasped by the ideas that make up the real world. Both tend to reinforce an interpretation of knowing as passive, as receiving. Kant's analysis in the *Critique of Pure Reason* demonstrated the activity of the mind and of the imagination in knowing. It is this activity, more fully set forth in its temporal and social contexts, that Royce is describing when he describes the process of interpretation.

The relationship of the one and the many, of the individual to his social context, is described by the process of interpretation. It is not described by portraying each individual knower as an atomic unit and the world as an aggregate of such units, nor by portraying the world as one substance of which individual knowers are modifications.

> Conception is often denounced, in our day, as "sterile." But perception, taken by itself, is intolerably lonesome. And every philosophy whose sole principle is perception invites us to dwell in a desolate wilderness where neither God nor man exists. For whether either God or man is in question, interpretation is demanded. (2:151)

This provides the foundation for Royce's discussion of a community of interpretation and his identification of the being of God with such a community.

THE COMMUNITY OF INTERPRETATION

Royce has described the triadic nature of interpretation. Though the comparison of two things may at first appear dyadic, there must always be a third by which the similarity or difference between the two is interpreted. The implicit question in any comparison is always "Wherein lies the difference or similarity between A and B?" Likenesses and differences are occasions for interpretation, but they are not their own interpretations. The search is always for a third in the light of which the relation between the two is understood. This third then also needs to be interpreted to another or to oneself at a later stage. Royce was always sensitive to the identification of his thought with Hegelian idealism and there is an obvious affinity between the triadic character of interpretation that he has described and the Hegelian dialectic. He anticipates the critics who might attempt to dismiss this as a restating of the Hegelian process, though he does not deny the affinity.

> I reply, further, that Peirce's concept of interpretation defines an extremely general process, of which the Hegelian dialectical triadic process is a very special case. Hegel's elementary illustrations of his own processes are ethical and historical. Peirce's theory of comparison is quite as well illustrated by explicitly social instances. . . . Peirce's theory with its explicitly empirical origin and its very exact logical working out, promises new light on matters which Hegel left profoundly problematic. (2:185–86)

Royce's voluntarism is also present in the idea of interpretation. Interpretation is an act. He states his agreement with William James's description of an idea as an active process or a "leading" (2:181). Royce can then speak of the will to interpret. The will to interpret is the impetus behind the activity of knowing. The will to interpret is also the will to autonomy. It is expressed in Kant's image near the beginning of the first critique when he speaks of calling nature to the witness stand and compelling it to answer questions that he puts to it, and in Hegel's contention that the essence of the human spirit is freedom. It is the will to judge for oneself in matters of knowing.[20]

> When we consider the inner life of the individual man, the Will to Interpret appears, then, as the will to be self-possessed.[21]

Royce does not develop this point further, but it is presupposed in his discussion of the community. Interpretation of one's world is correlative with possessing oneself. As knowledge of oneself comes about through the appropriation and interpretation of one's own experience and of the responses of others, the will to interpret is the will to possess oneself or to discover or create one's own identity. The unity experienced by an individual self is the unity of his world as he interprets it.

Interpretation is a continual process, but it is not open-ended in the sense of never being determinate. It is always determinate, and may bring us to understand something that is exact. Royce uses several examples here. By the method of induction it is often possible to discover processes or laws that can be stated clearly and that provide an interpretation of the phenomena. But a discovery that a conclusion is implied by certain premises is also an interpretation. The theories of any given science are the result of continual interpretation and reinterpretation by the community. Reinterpretation is always possible. The theory of relativity provides a totally new interpretation of classical mechanics. But that does not mean that classical mechanics was not determinate and was open-ended. It provided a unification of evidence and conception that required modification after new evidence had accumulated. But unification is possible both for the scientific community and for the individual self.

> One who compares a pair of his own ideas may attain, if he is successful, that vision of unity, that grade of self-possession, which we have now illustrated. (2:204)

In fact some such unity, some knowledge of oneself as an integral person, is necessary at each moment if one is to remain healthy. This is what is meant by ego strength. This unity is threatened in persons who have weak egos. It is lacking in the schizophrenic.

This experience of personal unity provides the ideal or

the model for the goal of all interpretation that an individual attempts. He has an experience of being able to interpret the world in a unified way as he interprets past experiences to his present and future self. It is this experience that serves as a model when he attempts to successfully interpret the world to others.

> When I compare two ideas of my own, the luminous self-possession which then, for a time, may come to be mine, forms for me an ideal of success in interpretation. This ideal I can attain only at moments. But these moments are a model for all my interpretations to follow. (2:205)

This is an important point. It is addressed directly to the topic of this investigation. The experience of unity in the individual's own interpretation of his experience serves as the model and the goal for reaching unity with others.

Perhaps this can be described in another way. If a person is to interpret idea A to person B, it will be necessary for him to appropriate idea A or somehow make it his own in order that he may present it to B in a new form. A linguistic interpreter must first hear and grasp the message from the original speaker if he is to couch it in language that will be understood by the person to whom the message is addressed. A typist need not be an interpreter. A typist may just transcribe letters or words from draft to final copy with no appropriation or even notice of their meaning. An interpreter must appropriate what he is to interpret. He does not have to affirm it, but he must take it in and make it his.

When an individual interprets an idea or an event from his own past in the light of present experience, he has little trouble appropriating the idea or the event to be interpreted. It may be the case that in many sessions with a psychoanalyst he struggles to appropriate an event or idea of his own past. Under normal circumstances, however, this process of appropriation has been proceeding apace so that the event as he remembers it has been appropriated and is integrated in his view of his own history. Thus he is in a uniquely fortunate position to interpret this event in the light of his present experience. It may be more difficult for him to interpret this event to another person who does not share the same history. In order to do that he will have to describe the history that is relevant to the context of the event and try to enable the other to grasp it. In attempting to interpret the event to another he tries to fill in enough background information to approximate in the other the unity that he himself experiences.

Two persons may be working together to solve a complex puzzle that involves several variables and combinations. One person says "I see the solution." The other asks what it is. Then the first person proceeds either to recapitulate the steps through which he moved in reaching the solution, or somehow to portray the structure and the mutual relations of the different parts of the puzzle in order to interpret the solution to the other. He will try to approximate in the mind of his colleague the unity and closure that he himself experiences as the solution to the problem. His own experience of closure is the model that provides the goal toward which he aims in interpreting the solution to his colleague. Royce uses this experience as the basis for his assertion that the will to interpret creates a community of interpretation.

> The interpreter, the mind to which he addresses his interpretation, the mind which he undertakes to interpret,—all these appear, in our explicitly human and social world, as three distinct selves,—sundered by chasms which, under human conditions, we never cross, and contrasting in their inner lives in whatever way the motives of men at any moment chance to contrast.
> The Will to Interpret undertakes to make of these three selves a Community. In every case of ideally serious and loyal effort truly to interpret this is the simplest, but, in its deepest motives, the most purely spiritual of possible communities. Let us view that simple and ideal community as the interpreter himself views it, precisely in so far as he is sincere and truth-loving in his purpose as interpreter. (2:207–8)

> I seek unity with you. And since the same will to interpret you is also expressive of my analogous interests in all my other neighbors, what I here and now specifically aim to do is this: I

mean to interpret you to somebody else, to some other neighbor, who is neither yourself nor myself. Three of us, then, I seek to bring into the desired unity of interpretation. (2:209)

This community is one that arises out of voluntary activity. It is created. It is also the community that provides the possibility of knowing. The problem of the one and the many was manifested in Royce's earlier philosophy by his claim that there must be an Absolute in order to account for the possibility of knowledge and for the making of errors juxtaposed with his voluntarism and the assertion that individuals were differentiated by their wills and the deeds that they authored. Now these two seemingly conflicting claims have been brought together. The Absolute is not one that denies individuality but it is a community of individuals. Far from allowing no possibility of autonomy or the activity of the will in knowing, it is a community that both creates and is a creation of the will to interpret. This will is present in every individual and leads to a sharing of experience and knowledge.

The result is not an Absolute that obscures the status of individuals or absorbs them like drops in an ocean, as was suggested not only by *The Religious Aspect of Philosophy* but also by *The World and the Individual*. Royce is clear now that the community of interpretation is a community of individuals.

> For our functions as the mind interpreted, the mind to whom the other is interpreted, and the interpreter, would remain as distinct as they now are. There would be no melting together, no mystic blur, and no lapse into mere intuition. But for me the vision of the successful interpretation would simply be the attainment of my own goal as interpreter. This attainment would as little confound our persons as it would divide our substance. We should remain, for me, many, even when viewed in this unity. (2:210)

Royce here uses the language of the trinitarian dogma to speak of a unity of substance and a distinction of persons. This is a community of interpretation.

It is this goal, represented by the community of interpretation at which all men aim, and providing the basis for attaining a unity of knowledge, that is the common event in the future that provides an actual community of men now. Royce has earlier said that in order for a community to exist, it must be possible for selves to extend themselves ideally into the past and future; there must exist individuals with the power to communicate who are communicating to some extent, and these individuals must share at least one event in the past or the future ideal extensions of themselves. The community must also be related to will or purpose. Now Royce has described that community of interpretation which is the goal or the aim of knowing as an event aimed at by all men who seek to know. It is the goal or the purpose of the interpretation in which they engage. Thus this community, a goal to be striven for that always remains in the future and can only be approached asymptotically, becomes the basis for an actual community in the present. Only an ideal observer can comprehend that community of interpretation at which men aim in knowing, but the function of that community as a goal for interpretation serves to create a community of all seekers after truth.

This goal is one that commands our loyalty. All forms of true loyalty involve the loyalty toward a community of interpretation. The fidelity toward language on which communication depends within a given society, the loyalty to certain agreed-upon procedures and conventions that creates the fabric of a scientific community and allows for the pursuit of truth, the loyalty to abide by certain legal and moral codes that enables persons with diverse interests and goals to live together in a society are all dependent upon loyalty to a community of interpretation. It is here that the one and the many, the quest and the goal, diverse ways of approaching knowledge, all come together. The community of interpretation provides a unity of knowing and acting, of intellect and will, of individual and absolute. This, says Royce, is what is meant by the being of God.

And, if, in ideal, we aim to conceive the divine nature, how better can we conceive it than in the form of the Community of Interpretation, and above all in the form of the Interpreter, who interprets all to all, and each individual to the world, and the world of spirits to each individual.

In such an interpreter, and in his community, the problem of the One and the Many would find its ideally complete expression and solution. (2:219)

God is conceived as the ideal interpreter and as the community of interpretation that is the ideal or goal of all interpretation. This ideal is visible to the imagination because of the unity of a community of interpretation that is experienced within the self. Thus the experience of the unity of plural roles within the self provides the model for the experience of the unity of all plurality in knowing and willing, which is God.

Royce proceeds to argue that the real world as experienced and described by men is an object of interpretation. He has already argued that knowledge in the scientific community is dependent upon the mutual criticism and interpretation of insights and hypotheses of individuals in that community. He alludes to the realm of law in which an advocate or interpreter is employed to represent a cause of one person to another. Any social quest for truth involves this process of interpretation.

Consider the ordinary case of two persons trying to establish a common object of their perception. Royce uses an example of two men who are rowing together in the same boat. Both men perceive the boat, each has his own idea of the boat, and both believe that it is the same boat, but this belief is an interpretation. Each can verify his own idea of the boat. Neither can verify the other's idea of the boat. The fact that they perceive a common boat is a belief or interpretation. It is not a fact to which they can have immediate access either through intuition or conception. Neither person would be able to verify that the boat was common regardless of how long they investigated or rowed. If their common interpretation is true, it can only be founded on the fact that they form a community of interpretation and are believing what would be seen to be true if that community reached its goal. In other words, they are believing what might be seen by an ideal observer if he could share both perspectives and interpret those perspectives to himself, but what is not accessible to either of them. Royce's criticism of the pragmatists was that they usually interpreted the boat as a common object but that the verifying experience could not be defined in their terms.[22]

Pragmatism is represented by Royce as implying that all knowledge ultimately rests on clear and immediate perceptions as the touchstone or criterion for truth. He cites James's reference to ideas possessing only "credit-value" that must one day be redeemed for their "cash-value" in experience. This appeal to direct intuition in experience as the secure ground in which all ideas must be rooted is contrasted with Plato's emphasis on conception, where all knowledge must be rooted in the realm of ideas. Over against these extreme appeals to direct empirical intuition and to absolute conceptions, Royce places the notion of interpretation as mediator between ideas and raw experience.

Royce's representation of pragmatism is inadequate. James did not formulate a theory of interpretation, and his terminology is not always precise. The image of cash and credit value, in conjunction with his constant reference to the empirical testing of ideas, might suggest that all knowledge was to be judged with reference to the immediate certainty of experience. This implication arises from his polemic against various forms of idealism.

> No particular results, then, so far, but only an attitude of orientation, is what the pragmatic method means. *The attitude of looking away from first things, principles, "categories," supposed necessities; and of looking toward last things, fruits, consequences, facts.*[23] (Original emphasis)

James emphasizes consequences and fruits, but Royce writes of this position as if it were a kind of logical positivism, a referral of all ideas to the experience of simple facts, much like Bertrand Russell's concept of knowledge by acquaintance or the doctrine presented in Wittgenstein's *Tractatus*.

James was led to his formulation of the pragmatic method by rereading Peirce's early essays.[24] Peirce certainly did not have recourse to a fundamental intuition or perception that might serve as the criterion of all experience. Nor did James have such a criterion in mind. In the same essay from which the above statement is taken, James asserts that the pragmatic method is a never-ending process, and that the task of the pragmatist is to employ ideas in thought and action, and to discover their function in human life. It is not to see whether or not they lead us back to some direct intuition or perception.

> But if you follow the pragmatic method, you cannot look on any such word [e.g., *God, Reason, the Absolute*] as closing your quest. You must bring out of each word its practical cash-value, set it at work within the stream of your experience. It appears less as a solution, then, than as a program for more work, and more particularly as an indication of the ways in which existing realities may be *changed*.
>   *Theories thus become instruments, not answers to enigmas, in which we can rest.*[25] (Original emphasis)

This is not a view in which ideas obtain their meaning by reference to simple facts of experience. It is not the view of the *Tractatus,* but is similar to that of the *Philosophical Investigations*. Ideas have their meaning in *use*. The process of referring ideas back to experience is a never-ending process that appears very similar to Royce's doctrine of interpretation, though James has not described the triadic structure of that process, and has not presented a clear view of the logic involved, as did Peirce and Royce.

Perhaps "cash-value" is a misleading image. Royce takes it to mean a referral of theoretical notes to a stockpile of bullion or hard cash that is direct empirical perception. James seems rather to mean that the conceptual notes must be redeemed by functioning within the social economy as does cash, by their ability to facilitate transactions. The cash value of ideas is not a treasure house of directly experienced facts, but is the ability of those ideas to facilitate social transactions and to obtain a purchase on the world of our experience.

Whenever a person reports that he has found an object or discovered a fact, he is not reporting only a private experience and rearrangement of his own ideas but is making a public claim and thus is appealing to a community of interpretation. Though the procedure is not so formal as it is within a scientific community, the appeal is the same in common experience. Such an appeal always presupposes both the existence of a community of interpretation and also that the community will eventually reach its goal. In other words, it presupposes a community of interpretation and a real world such that the interpretation will eventually, in principle, reach closure.

Royce notes that philosophers who emphasize only conception are able to derive everything from one idea, such as Spinoza's idea of substance. Those who emphasize only perception search for that intuition, the vision of God, the positive revelation, or the apprehension that will provide immediacy and certainty. The immediate closure sought by both of these approaches is impossible because of the social and temporal character of interpretation. That closure can exist only in the ideal extension of the community of interpretation as it reaches its goal.

The real world is to be understood as the interpretation of the situation in which we find ourselves. Royce claims that reality always presents itself as an antithesis, or as a comparison. It presents itself as two terms that require a third for interpretation.

This antithesis may take different forms. It is the idea of present experience and the idea of the goal of experience.

When the antithesis is that between appearance and reality, the real world is the community of interpretation that is constituted by the two antithetical ideas and their interpreter. This is the basis of all metaphysics.

> If you succeed in reducing this antithesis to its simplest statement, the world-problem then becomes the problem of defining the mediating idea in terms of which this contrast or antithesis can be and is interpreted. If you define, however tentatively, such a mediating idea, and then offer the resulting interpretation of what the real world is, your philosophy becomes an assertion that the universe itself has the form and the real character of a community of interpretation. You have no reason for believing that there is any world whatever, except a reason which implies that some interpretation of the antithesis both exists and is true. A real and a true interpretation occur only in case the corresponding community exists and wins its goal.[26]

The will to interpret and the presuppositions that men make in assuming a common world are founded on the existence of a community of interpretation. Implicit in the will to interpret is a belief in the possibility of closure of that process of interpretation, even though that closure can never be directly experienced in finite existence. That existence must be ideally extended to the notion of an infinite community that wins its goal.

Voluntarism is an essential part of Royce's metaphysical theory. But he is anxious to dissociate his voluntarism from the pragmatism of James and his colleagues. In the process of drawing the appropriate distinctions Royce sketches approximately the same contrast that holds between the three types in a discussion of three different types of will. The first he describes as the will to live. Royce was influenced by the thought of Schopenhauer during his study in Germany at the beginning of his academic career. It was this influence that caused him continually to stress the voluntarism that distinguished his thought from that of many idealists. The will to live or self-assertion he saw as given its most adequate expression in the pragmatism that was then current. This will describes a self who is attuned to his own interests. He may acknowledge the existence of other men, but this acknowledgment is on the basis of an argument by analogy. From the fact of his own self-interest he infers the self-interest of others. This describes the position that has been delineated as individualistic.

The second type of will described by Royce is that of resignation. This he ascribes to those who treat the self in knowing as passive. This type may take two forms. It may emphasize either conception or perception. The example Royce uses is Bergson, who was currently exhorting philosophers and others to abandon themselves to pure perception. This attitude of resignation of the will is the orientation of the mystic. The mystical element is evident in Bergson's counsel to give oneself over to pure intuition, and it is evident in Tillich's description of allowing oneself to be grasped by the symbol that resigns itself, in the sense that it becomes completely transparent to that to which it points and in which it participates. While pragmatism embodies the will to live and the will of each individual entity to be autonomous, this type embodies the will of the individual to resign itself and to be absorbed into the whole of which it is a part.

Over against both of these types Royce sets the notion of will as loyalty. Loyalty embraces both autonomy and fidelity. It involves the recognition of both dependence and independence in the human situation. It results neither in the lonesome self attuned only to its own interests nor in the self resigning itself to the whole of which it is a part and seeking its center outside of itself. This loyalty discovers its true object in the world conceived as a community of interpretation.

Royce includes an interesting brief discussion of the problem of other minds as the key problem of social knowledge and a test case of one's position regarding truth and the universe. He briefly sketches the pragmatist's contention that knowledge of other minds is founded on an argument from analogy. I have direct experience of my own inner states. When I observe certain behavior, certain facial expressions and gestures in others that I know to be similar to behavior of my own that is correlated with certain inner states, I postulate the appropriate inner states in the other to accompany the behavior that I observe.

But this is not the case. How often do I view my own facial expressions? I do not "observe" certain inner states of my own and "observe" my facial expressions, correlate them and then make an analogical jump to posit such inner states in others on the basis of the same facial expressions. I do not observe my facial expressions at all, except perhaps occasionally in the mirror. My most important knowledge of my own expressive movements comes to me secondhand from the responses of others. I have much more direct knowledge of the expressions of others than I do of my own. And Royce has earlier argued that I do not first experience my inner state as anger and then argue out to the object of that anger. I experience someone as disappointing or despicable or blameworthy. It is only by a process of reflection, a process that takes some time to develop in the child, that I am able after the fact to describe my state as that of anger. This does not describe an immediate intuition but is the product of a sophisticated reflexive move. The argument by analogy from one's own privileged experience of his inner states and his expressive movements does not describe the way in which others are known.

Royce's denial that we observe our own expressions and behavior, and then attribute affective states or intentions to ourselves on the basis of those observations, is both less convincing and more peripheral to his argument than his notion that we have no immediate intuition of our inner states. If Royce had reflected on James's discussion of emotion in *The Principles of Psychology*, he might have perceived the centrality of interpretation in the James-Lange theory of emotion. James argued that emotion consists of observation of our own behavior and psychological states. Others have amended this theory to take account of our interpretations of that behavior and those states. Royce implies that we are not engaged in constant observation of ourselves because we rarely stand in front of mirrors. There are, however, much more pervasive and subtle forms of self-perception, and many substitutes for mirrors.[27]

The role of observation of bodily states and the consequences of one's own behavior is underemphasized by Royce, though his theoretical perspective allows for a more sophisticated account of such processes of interpretation than could be given in the context of either of the first two types. Royce's idealistic bias causes him to focus more on interpretations of memories and expectations than on interpretations of bodily states and behavior. For Royce, the object of an interpretation is always another mind, or an object that is a sign for another mind. This focus on the interpretation of ideas rather than on interpretation of the physical world may have played a role in his distorted view of pragmatism. It appears that James's enthusiasm for scientific investigation led Royce to conclude that James understood raw experience to be a touchstone to which all knowledge must be referred. The pragmatic method as described by Peirce and James, however, gives a much greater role to interpretation in the process of scientific inquiry than Royce's allusions to the pragmatists would suggest.

Royce provides his own description of the way in which other minds are known. The experience on which that knowledge is founded is the experience of a group of ideas that appear to have no interpretation. The self first tries to make sense out of such a collection of ideas. When it finds that it is unable to provide an interpretation of those ideas as its own in relation to its own memory and present experience, it hypothesizes an interpreter who is able to provide an interpretation that will integrate these ideas with its own. The hypothetical interpreter is the other self. This process rests on the conviction that every set of ideas has an interpretation, or as Royce has said, that the world is its own interpretation.

> The reason, then, for "postulating your mind" is that the ideas which your words and movements have aroused within me are not my own ideas, and cannot be interpreted in terms of my own ideas, while I actually hold, as the fundamental hypothesis of my social consciousness, that all contrasts of ideas have a real interpretation and are interpreted.[28]

This sounds like the argument of an idealist, and it is. But it also expresses the social character of knowing and the fidelity to a community of interpretation that underlies all knowledge.

Royce relates this fidelity to the interpretive community to the maxim that other persons ought to be treated as ends.

> You are not a mere extension by analogy of my own will to live. I do not, for the sake merely of such analogy, vivify your perceived organism. *You are an example of the principle whose active recognition lies at the basis of my only reasonable view of the universe. As I treat you, so ought I to deal with the universe. As I interpret the universe, so, too, in principle, should I interpret you.* (2: 322–23; original emphasis)

Another self should be treated as an end even as the universe is treated as an end, as a community that claims loyalty and that reaches its goal. Another self is also treated as an object of loyalty and is treated as one that reaches its goal of unity. Another self is to be treated as a unit with its own integrity, with a certain closure, though there is no way for us to experience the integrity, the unity of interpretation, that is that self. This attitude of respect and loyalty toward another self is related by Royce to the Pauline counsel of charity. It is the loyal will toward life in and through the spirit of community.

GOD AND COMMUNITY

There are few passages in *The Problem of Christianity* that are explicitly about God, and yet these passages suggest that Royce is proposing a conception of God that differs from his discussion of the Absolute in his earlier work. In the preface to this work he says:

> In spirit I believe my present book to be in essential harmony with the bases of the philosophical idealism set forth in various earlier volumes of my own, and especially in the work entitled "The World and the Individual" (published in 1899–1901). On the other hand, the present work contains no mere repetition of my former expressions of opinion. (1:xviii–xix)

There is no mention of the Absolute in *The Problem of Christianity,* or of the involved mathematical argument for the relation between finite and infinite that is contained in the "Supplementary Essay" to *The World and the Individual.* These abstract conceptions have given way to the social conceptions of interpretation and community.

In one passage where he speaks most directly about his new conception of the divine nature, however, Royce appears unclear about whether God is to be conceived as the community of interpretation or as the ideal interpreter of that community. His earler notion of God as absolute Self has given way to a more concrete discussion of social relations, but the question of whether God himself is to be conceived as an individual person or as an organic model of social relations remains open. In this important passage he identifies God both as the ideal interpreter and as the community of interpretation.

> And, if, in ideal, we aim to conceive the divine nature, how better can we conceive it than in the form of the Community of Interpretation, and above all in the form of the Interpreter, who interprets all to all, and each individual to the world, and the world of spirits to each individual.
> In such an interpreter, and in his community, the problem of the One and Many would find its ideally complete expression

and solution. The abstract conceptions and the mystical intuitions would be at once transcended, and illumined, and yet retained and kept clear and distinct, in and through the life of one who, as interpreter, was at once servant to all and chief among all, expressing his will through all, yet, in his interpretations, regarding and loving the will of the least of these his brethren. In him the Community, the Individual, and the Absolute would be completely expressed, reconciled, and distinguished. (2:219–20)

Although in this quotation God is identified both as the Community and as the ideal interpreter, the emphasis seems to fall on God as the interpreter. But the suggestion throughout the work is that Royce's earlier conception of God as absolute has now become more firmly rooted in social experience. While he attempted earlier to provide mathematical arguments for the existence of a concrete infinite,[29] he now discovers the infinite in his analysis of interpretation and the resulting community. The identification of God with the community is not merely a passing remark. The community of interpretation provides the conception of the infinite that takes the place of the earlier Absolute, and that is God. Royce also interprets the history of Christianity as one in which God is identified with such a community:

Christianity is characterized not only by the universality of the ideal community to which, in its greatest deeds and ages, it has, according to its intent, been loyal; but also by the depth and by the practical intensity and efficacy of the love towards this community which has inspired its most representative leaders and reformers; and, finally, by the profoundly significant doctrines and customs to which it has been led in the course of its efforts to identify the being of its ideal community with the being of God.[30]

In order to understand this identification of God with both the ideal interpreter and his community it is necessary to remember that for Royce every personal self is a community, and communities are persons. Royce has argued this by attending directly to the issue of unity. He has argued that the self is not a datum. It is an interpretation that unites various events, perceptions and conceptions contributed by past and present experience. The self is not an atom, but is itself a unity in plurality. It is a community. Royce has also given considerable attention to the way in which communities are persons. A community has a history and it also has a goal or a purpose. A community is the construction of successive interpretations, and the need for interpretation never ends. When Royce identifies the being of God with the community of interpretation, then, the issue of the relation between the personal and the impersonal has already been built into his discussion of self and community. It is not only in God that some such identity is necessary. A person is always the result of an interpretation that presupposes community.

> If by person you mean the morally detached individual man, then the community,—the Kingdom of Heaven, is indeed superpersonal. If, by person, you mean a live unity of knowledge and of will, of love and of deed,—then the community of the Kingdom of Heaven is a person on a higher level than is the level of any human individual; and the Kingdom of Heaven is at once within you, and above you,—a human life, and yet a life whose tabernacles are built on a Mount of Transfiguration. (1:352)

The Will to Interpret is a triadic relation that is composed of three minds. One mind attempts to interpret a second to a third. This process of interpretation involves a serious and loyal effort to make of these three selves a community. When this process involves my interpretation of something in my memory to my present and future self, this is the interpretation of my own unity as a person. The community that is constructed in this process is my self. When the three members of the interpretive process are different individuals, the community that is constructed is larger than that of one personal self, and is a social community. But both are unities forged by the process of interpretation out of a plurality of individual minds, whether those minds are all "mine" or belong to different bodies and interpretations.

It is important to look closely at Royce's argument for the identification of God with both the community of interpretation and its interpreter. There are two major steps to Royce's argument. The first is the establishment of the notion of the Community of Interpretation as the ideal goal of the process of interpretation, and its identification with the idea of God. The second is the metaphysical claim that such a goal and its interpreter actually exist.

As Royce develops the notion of interpretation, he notes that it differs from both perception and conception in two ways: (1) it is an endless social process, and (2) it is a relation that not only involves three terms, but brings those terms into a determinate order. It is this second point that is particularly significant for the identification of God with the community of interpretation. In the dyadic relation of encounter between two persons, the two terms of the relation are immediately present to each other, and the relation is symmetric. The triadic relation of interpretation, however, is an asymmetric relation. The order in which interpreter, object of interpretation, and person to whom the interpretation is addressed are related is a determinate order. When the order is varied, a different event is described. The paradigm of the asymmetry of the interpretive process is given by Royce's definition of the temporal order as an order of possible interpretation.

> In sum, if we view the world as everywhere and always recording its own history, by processes of aging and weathering, or of evolution, or of stellar and nebular clusterings and streamings, we can simply define the time order, and its three regions,— past, present, future,—as an order of possible interpretation. That is, we can define the present as, potentially, the interpretion of the past to the future. (2:147)

Royce employs this notion of the asymmetric character of the relation to demonstrate that while the process of interpretation may be endless, the form of the relation is determinate. He draws analogies with the process of mathematical deduction in which a certain determinate form can be given to the process, even though the theorems that can be deduced from a given set of axioms may be endless in number. Though the theorems may be relative to the axioms with which one begins, the determinate form of the process can be stated with exactitude and absolute determination. If one begins with these axioms, then it is possible to deduce these particular conclusions. Similarly, Royce suggests, the process of interpretation has a determinate form that is not relative to the particular object of interpretation or to the specific persons involved.

The process of interpretation also has a goal or ideal to be aimed at, which again is independent of any particular persons or signs that might be involved. That is the goal of unity. My experience of interpreting my own ideas to myself, which occasionally is accompanied by a fleeting sense of complete clarity, provides an ideal of success in the process of interpretation (2:205). I can never enjoy the same degree of success in interpreting another mind, because I do not have the access to that person's past that I have to my own (at least under normal conditions). That experience of clarity serves as the goal of all interpretation. It is the goal of unity of the mind that is interpreted and the mind to whom the interpretation is being made, shared by the interpreter who mediated between them.

Royce claims, then, that even though the particular persons involved in the processes of interpretation are always changing and the process is an endless one, two determinate and absolute truths can be known about that process. The first is its structure or form, and the second is its goal. The form of the process is triadic, and the goal is the forging of a community made up of the three persons involved. This community is a social one that does not blur the individual members. Since each of the members engaged in the interpretive process aims at the ideal of unity, there is an event in the future that is common to all three persons. That is the event of the successful completion of the interpretation. As noted above, the crucial characteristic of a community is the necessity for the individuals to share a common event in either memory or anticipation. Here the event is in the future, as the goal of the process of interpretation.

In this community, which is the ideal goal of all processes of interpretation, the interpreter assumes the chief role (2:216). As mediator, he gives his spirit to the community. He has actively created the interpretation, and yet he has also conformed himself to the sign to be interpreted and to the mind to which he is addressing the interpretation. His spirit unites by being both lord and servant.

When we return now to Royce's comment that the best way to conceive the divine nature, in ideal, is "in the form of the Community of Interpretation, and above all in the form of the Interpreter," we can see that he is formulating a version of the classical trinitarian doctrine of God. The ideal form and the ideal goal of the process of interpretation are determinate; the form is triadic and asymmetric, and the goal is a community of interpretation permeated by the spirit of the interpreter. This provides a demythologized formulation of the doctrine of the triune character of God, in which the persons are distinct, are related in a determinate order, and are members of a community drawn together by the spirit of the mediator. Royce's intention in this volume is to draw the philosophical implications of religious experience, and particularly of Christianity. This identification of the ideal notion of God with the community and its interpreter is a central part of that task.

The next thing that must be said about this conception of the divine nature is that it is, as yet, an ideal. It is a possible interpretation. This does not mean that it is not real. On the contrary, the self is an interpretation, as is the real world. But an interpretation must be judged as to its validity on the basis of reflection and experience. Royce profoundly disagreed with what he took to be the position of James and the pragmatists, that any idea that served a purpose or fulfilled a need was therefore valid. This view also suffers from Royce's inability to see the implicit interpretive character of the pragmatic theory of truth, but it was a position from which Royce wanted to distinguish himself. The need for a coherent theory of the universe enables us to imagine an ideal conception of the divine nature. But that ideal must have the support of experience and logic. Immediately after his identification of the ideal conception of the divine nature with the community and its interpreter, Royce stresses this point:

> This, to be sure, is, at this point of our discussion, still merely the expression of an ideal, and not the assertion of a metaphysical proposition. But in the Will to Interpret, the divine and the human seem to be in closest touch with each other. . . . Merely to define such ideas is not to solve the problems of metaphysics. But it is to remove many obstacles from the path that leads towards insight. (2:220–21)

In the chapter immediately following his statement of the ideal conception of God, Royce outlines his metaphysics of interpretation. Here he provides a reconstruction of the notion of the "real world."

> *By the "real world" we mean simply the "true interpretation" of this our problematic situation.* No other reason can be given than this for believing that there is any real world at all. From this one consideration, vast consequences follow. (2:264–65; original emphasis)

These consequences include an argument for the existence of the real world, and for the validity of the conception of God as the Community of Interpretation and its Interpreter. The argument presented in this chapter is intended to demonstrate the actuality of the ideal that arises from the will to interpret, or from the need for a coherent universe.

Royce's fundamental point is that the problem of reality consists in the comparison of two essential ideas. These ideas are (1) the idea of present experience, and (2) the idea of the goal of experience. The contrast between the two can take different forms, and each form will yield a different antithesis, which must be interpreted. For instance, in the ethical form, the contrast is between the ideal and the actual. In epistemology it is between knowledge and ignorance, and in the religious consciousness the same antithesis is illustrated by the contrasts between nature and grace, good and evil, and God and the world. The problem presented by these antitheses is the world problem.

Metaphysically, this contrast is between appearance and reality. So the metaphysical question is: what is the interpretation of this contrast? Royce's answer is that the real world is that solution. Every metaphysics takes the form of offering such a solution. Every philosopher offers an interpretation of the world problem. But suppose that there is no solution, so that philosophy is without meaning? Here Royce employs a variant form of his famous argument for the existence of the Absolute on the grounds of the necessity of accounting for error.[31] The argument has changed now, however, and is rooted in a social and temporal interpretation of the process of knowing. If it is proposed that there is no solution to the world problem, such a proposal has the same status as other hypotheses. It can be verified only by an experience that would make it a solution in itself. If it were verified, it would be self-contradictory. There is no way to conceive of the world problem without a solution, just as there is no way to conceive of perception without interpretation. Therefore there must be a solution to the antithesis, or an interpretation that constitutes the real world.

This argument is formulated in terms that raise the suspicion of metaphysical sleight of hand. It can perhaps be better understood when it is appreciated not as a logical argument for a counter-intuitive position, but as the descriptive statement that it is impossible for experience to remain uninterpreted. In the individual case, this is a psychological impossibility. It is not only subjective, however, because interpretation is a public and social process. We cannot conceive of the possibility that there exists no true interpretation of the world.

Royce goes on to argue that an interpretation is real only if the appropriate community is real, and is true only if that community reaches its goal. Since he has shown that there must be a true interpretation of the world, even though that interpretation will never be reached since the process is endless, the correlative community must be real, though that also will never be complete in the finite order:

> In brief, then, the real world is the Community of Interpretation which is constituted by the two antithetic ideas, and their mediator or interpreter, whatever or whoever that interpreter may be. If the interpretation is a reality, and if it truly interprets the whole of reality, then the community reaches its goal, and the real world includes its own interpreter. *Unless both the interpreter and the community are real, there is no real world.*[32](Original emphasis)

The reality of the world is grounded in the possibility of its having an interpretation. This is quite similar to Kant's discussion of the ideas of pure reason and of the postulates of practical reason in the two critiques. God is not experienced directly. Both the first two types claim moments in which man experiences God immediately. The experiences of ecstasy and the transparency of symbol in the monistic type and the possibility of apprehending God in the individualistic type are conceived as immediate experience. Royce argues, however, that no experience is ever unmediated and that the unity that is God is arrived at in the same manner as I arrive at that unity which is myself. It is an interpretation of experience directed toward the end of understanding that experience.

THE MORAL BURDEN—
GUILT AND ATONEMENT

The foregoing analysis has focused on Royce's description of interpretation as a mode of cognition and of the community of interpretation as a metaphysical proposal. In his analysis of the Christian ideas that present themselves to modern man as a problem for interpretation, the problem of Christianity, Royce delineates not only the idea of the community and the church, but two other ideas that he takes to be essential to Christianity and that further illumine his conception of the relation between the individual and community and between man and God. These are the idea of the moral burden of the individual, corresponding to the classical Christian notion of original sin, and the idea of atonement.

Royce's description of the moral burden of the individual is an ingenious one and is an example of how deeply his philosophical conceptions are rooted in observation of the processes of growth in society. As was the case with his discussion of self-knowledge as conversation and interpretation, so also is his discussion of the moral burden of the individual; there is now much more data available from the social sciences in support of Royce's description than there was in his time. Even the work that was available at that time does not seem to have been familiar to Royce. He draws on Troeltsch at one point, but never mentions Durkheim, Weber, Marx, or Freud, some of whose work was available and would have been relevant to Royce's interests.

The moral burden, as Royce describes it, deals not with the conduct of men, but with their consciousness about their conduct. He begins with Paul's discussion of the divided self, and asks what this division might be. It is, he decides, the conflict of two loyalties. These are the loyalty of a person to himself and his loyalty to the law, or to the community. But the important thing is that this conflict is not an accidental one. Moral self-consciousness is bred in situations of social conflict. The development of an autonomous ego arises out of situations in which selves set themselves over against each other, negotiate, become conscious of their own autonomy, and discover or create themselves as individuals. The adolescent strives to differentiate himself primarily from home and family, but he is also concerned to differentiate himself from all others, to be responded to as an individual, because he is seeking to establish his autonomy. This autonomy must be established psychologically, economically, morally. The individual is seeking his own identity. This process is essential for an individual to become a healthy person, to establish his own independence, and to make his own decisions. It is essential for anyone in order for him to become a responsible citizen in a society. But it is exactly the process of cultivation, of providing a context in which persons can develop to become autonomous citizens with their own egos, that arouses and increases self-will. As the individual becomes a fuller citizen in the society, he becomes more resistant to external authority. As the social order develops, both individualism and collectivism intensify each other. Paul's divided self is descriptive of this conflict.

> On the one hand, as reasonable being, I say, "I ought to submit, for law is mighty; and I would not, if I could, bring anarchy." So much I say, if I am indeed successfully trained. But I will not obey with the inner man. For I am the being of inalienable individual rights, of unconquerable independence. I have my own law in my own members, which, however I seem to obey, is at war with the social will. I am the divided self. The more I struggle to escape through my moral cultivation, the more I discern my divided state. Oh, wretched man that I am! (1:150–51)

The more complex and developed a society becomes, the more the conflict between individual autonomy and communal cooperation is exacerbated. Each side of the conflict is intensified.

From the studies of anthropologists it can be seen that there is little or no sense of the individual self in very primitive societies. The primary unit is the tribe or clan or the extended family. As society becomes differentiated in institutions, in its symbol system, and in personal relations, individuals begin to develop images of themselves that are not identical with their roles in the society. The historical consciousness of Israel, the consciousness of the freedom of individual citizens from the culture of classical Greece, and the emphasis upon salvation or conversion of the individual in Christianity combined to produce a differentiation and a sense of the self as having its own history that was not possible earlier.

As the hierarchy of medieval society, which was identified with the hierarchy in the chain of being, began to break down toward the end of the Middle Ages and serfs were able to obtain their freedom and become citizens of the small towns and cities that arose, the way was paved for a new breakthrough in a conception of the individual as free, able to rebel, and responsible for his own salvation. He alone now read the Bible and stood before God, without the mediation of the institution of the church and priesthood. This breakthrough was symbolized by Martin Luther and was complemented by the emphasis upon individual creativity and personality in Renaissance art and literature. Erikson's study of Luther suggests that it was impossible for a crisis of identity of the kind that Luther experienced to occur before the differentiation accompanying the breakdown of the feudal structure, the rise of nominalism in the later Middle Ages, Cartesian doubt, and the Renaissance.[33] Each of these attests to a differentiation that was taking place in many spheres of the culture.

This differentiation and assertion of the freedom and even isolation of the individual led to a new formulation of the basis for community. The theory of the social contract could not have developed in the medieval context. That theory presupposes a conception of individuals who are autonomous and independent entities. Such individuals come together and negotiate a contract for governing themselves. Government is not ascribed according to some hierarchy that is supposed to follow the order of the cosmos or of being. Thus the assertion of individual autonomy and the possibility of a new form of cooperation and community arise together. This process of differentiation accompanied by new forms of more complex integration can be observed and studied in every case of social development. It can be observed in the development of a self from infancy to adulthood, in the development of institutions of society from primitive social systems to complex industrial society, in the development of language from primitive speech to the present, and in the development of small groups from the initial meeting to their dissolution.

It is this conflict that comes from differentiation and from the development of a complex society that Royce described as the moral burden of the individual. Issues of establishing one's identity are much more difficult to deal with in contemporary society than they were for primitive man. On the other hand, the possibilities and resources for contemporary man are much more numerous. If a primitive individual developed in a way that was out of step with the norm of his tribe, he might have been banished or have experienced such ostracism that he could no longer live. In places characterized by little differentiation and pluralism and where conservative norms hold sway, it is very difficult for an individual to assert his own autonomy in matters of faith and morals. Differentiation allows for pluralism and also allows for more complex forms of cooperation and community. It strengthens the desire for cooperation and a more complex society, while it also strengthens the individual will.

This burden can be met only by loyalty to an all-embracing community that includes within it individual diversity. This loyalty is also more differentiated and complex than the kind of devotion that might be experienced in primitive society or in the case of an infant. It is not blind devotion to a cause, but the kind of loyalty appropriate to an autonomous individual who self-consciously devotes himself to a cause.

> Loyalty, if it comes at all, has the value of a love which does not so much renounce the individual self as devote the self, with all its consciousness and its powers, to an all-embracing unity of individuals in one realm of spiritual harmony.[34]

It is not blind devotion or an instance of the self becoming transparent to and surrendering itself to a center outside itself, as is suggested in the monistic type and in the experience of the mystic. This renunciation of the individual self is most fully represented in the goal of *nirvana* in some forms of Buddhism. But the loyalty of which Royce speaks is not self-renunciation, but the conscious and active devotion of oneself to a cause that is possible only for the self-conscious and autonomous individual. This loyalty is grace.

Royce then proceeds to describe not what is depicted by the doctrine of original sin, but the guilt that is felt when someone feels that he has committed a sinful act. Royce is interested not in any act that was committed but in the consciousness of having sinned. With allusion to Matthew Arnold, he considers briefly the counsel of liberal religion that such guilt should be forgotten and left behind. Again, however, Royce is interested in the psychological and sociological implications of such a consciousness. If grace is understood in terms of loyalty, then the counterpart for understanding sin is betrayal. Royce takes the ideal case of the traitor as a paradigm for guilt. The traitor is one who has found a cause to which he has devoted himself, has loved this cause, and yet has betrayed it.

The possibility of betrayal arises correlatively with the possibility of loyalty. If an individual and society have reached a degree of complexity such that no blind devotion but self-conscious and voluntary loyalty is possible, then a betrayal of that loyalty is also possible.

> One who has found his cause, if he has a will of his own, can become a conscious and deliberate traitor. One who has found his loyalty is indeed, at first, under the obsession of the new spirit of grace. But if, henceforth, he lives with a will of his own, he can, by a wilful closing of his eyes to the light, *become* disloyal. (1:252)

For such a person, to forget the betrayal and go on as if nothing had happened is not possible. He has betrayed not only an external authority, but a cause that was his own and to which he had devoted himself.

Royce then considers several of the traditional theories of the atonement. These theories may be correlated with the types of this study. The description of reconciliation offered by the monistic type is reunion with the ground of one's being. It is for the infant to be taken up again into the arms of the mother. Love and warmth are still present. It is the notion of forgiveness. One of Tillich's most famous sermons had as its message: "Accept the fact that you are accepted." The sinner is accepted as he is and is absorbed into the fold, into the ground in which he participates.

It is appropriate for the infant to know that he is still accepted even though he has done something to disappoint the mother. But this is not adequate for the traitor. The person who has betrayed his own cause needs not only the reassurance that he is still embraced as a part of the whole, needs not only to hear the words "You are accepted." His betrayal was not only a betrayal of the ground of his being, but of himself as an individual.

Atonement has also been described in terms of the penal satisfaction of Christ. Christ satisfies the wrath of God and we are judged by God to be justified. Thus the wrath of another, initially directed toward us, is pacified. This also is no reconciliation. This is a forensic decision that might be appropriate to the relationship between father and son, or between king and subject. If the subject has incurred the wrath of his ruler, he will be glad to have that wrath pacified by whatever intervention of mercy is offered to him. Priests and princesses often perform such roles in the stories of monarchs and their subject. But this pacification of an angry judge is something external and accidental. It does not deal with the consciousness of the traitor that he has betrayed the cause of the community that is the object of his own loyalty. He is not seeking a forensic judgment of pardon; he is seeking real reconciliation.

No reconciliation can be found. But it can be created, says

Royce. It is possible that new relationships and a new community can be created on the occasion of and on the basis of the treason. Experiences of mistrust and disappointment in the life of parents and children, of man and wife, of friends and colleagues may sometimes provide the occasion for new communication, for an understanding not possible previously, and for the experience of sharing that provides a new trust and a new basis for community. The naive and unblemished relationships that were present before the deed occurred can no longer be recovered, but perhaps the conflict and disappointment can be dealt with and a new relationship created. This, according to Royce, is atonement. It is the triumph of the creative will.

> *The world as transformed by this creative deed, is better than it would have been had all else remained the same, but had that deed of treason not been done at all.* (1:307–8; original emphasis)

This is reconciliation through the creation of a new community. It is not justification of the individual as in the second type, or restoration to the state that existed before the betrayal occurred as in the first type, but it is the creation of a community that did not exist previously and that could not have come into being without the betrayal. This is an emphasis upon the Christian doctrine of sanctification or the creation of a new spiritual existence, rather than individual justification or restoration of the part to the whole in which it participates. Atonement is sanctification and the creation of new community.

Royce understands such creativity to be so deeply rooted in human experience that the doctrine of atonement would have had to be invented if there were no Christianity.

> The human aspect of the Christian idea of atonement is based upon such motives that, if there were no Christianity and no Christians in the world, the idea of atonement would have to be invented, before the higher levels of our moral existence could be fairly understood. (1:271)

The possibility of such reconciliation is a practical postulate of the human community.

> *No baseness or cruelty of treason so deep or so tragic shall enter into our human world, but that loyal love shall be able in due time to oppose to just that deed of treason the fitting deed of atonement.* (1:322; original emphasis)

God has been described as the community of interpretation ideally extended. Thus the being of God increases with this process of atonement.

Reality is social and temporal. The self is a *polis* and develops in correlation with its social context. A community is composed of selves and each individual self is also to be understood as a community. The being of God is not an Absolute that is removed from this process, but is the foundation and the goal of human knowing and purposeful activity. God is the community of interpretation that provides the ground for all interpretation.

> The universe, if my thesis is right, is a realm which is through and through dominated by social categories. Time, for instance, expresses a system of essentially social relations. The present interprets the past to the future. At each moment of time the results of the whole world's history up to that moment are, so to speak, summed up and passed over to the future for its new deeds of creation and of interpretation. I state this principle here in a simply dogmatic form, and merely as an example of what I have in mind when I say that the system of metaphysics which is needed to define the constitution of the world of interpretation must be the generalized theory of an ideal society. Not the Self, not the Logos, not the One, and not the Many, but the Community will be the ruling category of such a philosophy. (2:280–81)

Reality is not conceived as an undifferentiated whole nor as an aggregate of individual entities, but as a community composed of individuals who are united in a common aim.

NOTES

1. The interpretation of Royce in this chapter is indebted to John E. Smith, *Royce's Social Infinite* (New York: Liberal Arts Press, 1950) and J. Harry Cotton, *Royce on the Human Self* (Cambridge, Mass.: Harvard University Press, 1954).

2. Ludwig Wittgenstein, *Philosophical Investigations*, trans. G. E. M. Anscombe (New York: The Macmillan Company, 1953), pp. 94–96.

3. Farrer is more careful than some in avoiding the strong separation between persons and inanimate nature that is characteristic of many thinkers of the individualistic type. In Farrer's work the existentialist tradition, which has emphasized this dualism, is modified by the Thomistic tradition, in which both personal and impersonal entities are united under the rubric of substance.

4. Josiah Royce, *The Problem of Christianity* (New York: The Macmillan Company, 1913), 2: 17–18.

5. See the "Supplementary Essay" at the end of vol. 1 of Josiah Royce, *The World and the Individual* (New York: The Macmillan Company, 1899), pp. 473–588. Here Royce deals directly with the issue of the one and the many, particularly in conversation with and criticism of the work of F. H. Bradley.

6. Royce, *The Problem of Christianity*, vol. 2, chap. 13. Royce cites the intellectual community of scientists as an example of a community of interpretation.

7. *Ibid.*, 2: 114n.

8. Charles Sanders Peirce, "Questions Concerning Certain Faculties Claimed for Man" (1868), *Collected Papers*, ed. C. Hartshorne and P. Weiss (Cambridge, Mass.: Harvard University Press) 5: 213–63.

9. Austin Farrer, *Finite and Infinite*, 2d ed. (London: Dacre Press, 1959), p. ix.

10. Immanuel Kant, *Critique of Pure Reason*, trans. and ed. N. K. Smith (London: Macmillan and Company, 1933), pp. 244ff.

11. Royce believed, and made explicit mention of the fact, that Peirce's doctrine of interpretation and his attack on intuitive self-consciousness were not influenced by Hegel and German idealism. See *The Problem of Christianity*, 2: 116, 185–86. In college, however, Peirce had studied German philosophy, and had learned Kant's first critique "almost by heart." Paul Weiss, "Biography of Charles S. Peirce," *Perspectives on Peirce*, ed. R. J. Bernstein (New Haven, Conn.: Yale University Press, 1965), p. 2.

12 It is interesting to note that some of the basic insights of continental idealism have been extremely influential when propounded by someone standing within the Anglo-American tradition against a background of empiricism and positivism. Two works that are similar in style and format, being collections of aphorisms and brief considerations of topics, are Samuel Taylor Coleridge's *Aids to Reflection* and Ludwig Wittgenstein's *Philosophical Investigations*. Both quickly attracted a cult of followers. Much of the power of both may have come from the introduction into the empiricist or positivist atmosphere of Britain of some of the insights common in German idealism. The fusion of the two streams was important. Peirce's style has affinities with both of these works.

13. Peirce, "Questions Concerning Certain Faculties . . . ," pp. 225–37.

14. For a discussion of recent empirical studies of self-perception, and elaboration of this interpretation of emotion, see Wayne Proudfoot and Phillip Shaver, "Attribution Theory and the Psychology of Religion," *Journal for the Scientific Study of Religion* 14 (1975): 317–30.

15. Claude Lévi-Strauss, *Structural Anthropology*, trans. C. Jacobson and B. G. Schoepf (Garden City, N. Y.: Doubleday, 1967), pp. 161–80.

16. Royce, *The Problem of Christianity*, 2: 43.

17. Royce might well have pointed to recent discussions of the "recital of the acts of God" in Israel's tradition if he had been writing today. G. Ernest Wright, *God Who Acts* (London: Student Christian Movement Press, 1952), and Gerhard

von Rad, *Studies in Deuteronomy*, trans. D. Stalker (London: Student Christian Movement Press, 1956).

18. Royce, *The Problem of Christianity*, 2:40.

19. The process of interpretation is a third process, which is not reducible to James's distinction between cash value and credit value. *The Problem of Christianity*, 2:131–32.

20. Kant, *Critique of Pure Reason*, trans. N. K. Smith, p. 20; and Georg Wilhelm Friedrich Hegel, *Reason in History*, trans. R. S. Hartman (New York: Bobbs-Merrill, 1953), pp. 22ff.

21. *The Problem of Christianity*, 2:193.

22. Royce comments on the pragmatists:
Pragmatism, whose ideas, like those of the bewitched Galatians, are fain to be saved solely by their own "works," is, as I believe, quite unable to define in its own dyadic terms, the essentially spiritual sense in which any interpretation can be true and the sense in which any community of interpretation can reach its goal. . . . Yet their community, by hypothesis, is real. But if the real world contains the actual winning of the goal by the community, then the verifying experience is not definable in the terms which pragmatism uses. (*The Problem of Christianity*, 2:243–45).

23. William James, "What Pragmatism Means," *Pragmatism* (New York: Longmans, Green and Company, 1907), pp. 54–55.

24. See *Pragmatism*, p. 46, where James expresses his debt to Peirce's 1878 article, "How to Make Our Ideas Clear."

25. *Pragmatism*, p. 53.

26. Royce, *The Problem of Christianity*, 2:275–76.

27. For an account of current empirical studies and theoretical accounts stemming from James's theory, and emphasizing the interpretive character of self-knowledge, see Proudfoot and Shaver, "Attribution Theory and the Psychology of Religion."

28. Royce, *The Problem of Christianity*, 2:322.

29. "Supplementary Essay" in Royce, *The World and the Individual*, 1:473–588.

30. Royce, *The Problem of Christianity*, 1:194–95.

31. Josiah Royce, "The Possibility of Error," *The Religious Aspect of Philosophy* (Boston: Houghton, Mifflin and Company, 1885), pp. 384–435.

32. Royce, *The Problem of Christianity*, 2:269–70.

33. Erik Erikson, *Young Man Luther* (New York: W. W. Norton and Company, 1958).

34. *The Problem of Christianity*, 1:189.

5

Conclusion

A process of differentiation is occurring in which the
academic study of religion is being distinguished from its
theological, and particularly its Protestant, origins. Until
very recently, and to a large extent even at the present time,
scholarly attention to religions outside the Judeo-Christian
tradition has been confined to historical and textual criticism. While comparable historical attention has been given
to Jewish and Christian sources, the philosophy of religion
in the West has been devoted almost entirely to the
philosophical prolegomena to or analytic criticism of Christian (and occasionally Jewish) doctrines and beliefs. Some
would label much of what has gone on under the rubric of
philosophy of religion as Christian philosophy, or Jewish or
Buddhist philosophy.[1] But there has been very little
philosophical comparison of the doctrines and practices of
Oriental and Occidental traditions. Ninian Smart's *Reasons
and Faiths* is a noteworthy exception, and a study that provides some valuable guidelines for such comparisons.

There are good reasons for the hesitation of scholars to
enter into the comparative study of religious beliefs and
practices. Where it has been attempted in the past, distortions of some traditions in the service of justifying others
have often been the result. Missionaries and theologians,
for instance, have often engaged in crude comparisons of
Christian doctrines and customs with those of other

212

peoples. The comparisons and contrasts have often been so blatantly apologetic that any possibility of a sympathetic understanding of the other tradition has been precluded from the start. The purpose of such endeavors was usually to demonstrate either that the foreign tradition is one that is morally or spiritually inferior to that of the author, or to show that it is a repository for cryptic expressions of universal truths, truths more clearly and fully set out in the author's own tradition.

In reaction to the distortions of such apologetics, most scholars of religion have understandably refused to engage in comparisons, and have especially avoided comparisons with an evaluative dimension. The comparative study of religion has been limited primarily to historical and textual studies, the phenomenology of religious experience, and the sociological study of religious institutions. Increasingly, however, such studies have brought us to the point where it may be possible, and perhaps even necessary, to engage in the study of comparative religious world views. It is important to know the meaning of the word *nibbāna* in the classical Pali texts. But if Buddhism and Christianity are each a sophisticated and complex system of symbols and practices that are accessible to persons not nurtured in those traditions, then it becomes important to discover criteria by which the coherence and the implications of diverse world views can be compared and evaluated. If no such criteria are available, one is reduced to the appreciation of a number of religious systems that are finally incomparable. A person is born and raised in a specific tradition. If he or she should choose to convert or to appropriate aspects of another tradition, such a decision would be arbitrary. While there may be explanations for a person's being drawn to a particular view of the world, these could not be expressed in reasons or criteria that would necessarily be persuasive to anyone else. Religion, according to this view, is an expression of the natural lottery by which one is born into a particular culture, and of subjective preferences that are irrelevant to the knowledge we seek and criteria we adopt in other areas of our lives.

One of the difficulties involved in developing criteria for evaluating religious systems is the danger of unwittingly confusing descriptive and prescriptive tasks. Too often the criteria by which several world views have been compared have contained hidden assumptions about the superiority of a particular way of life. Evolutionary theories of morals and religion have posed special problems in this regard. Posing as descriptive theories, and perhaps having some validity as such, they often carry the implicit judgment that a particular stage is more mature, advanced, and to be preferred over earlier stages. Bellah is aware of this problem, and he explicitly denies that his stages carry a prescriptive connotation. It is clear, however, upon reading Bellah's analysis of religious evolution, that the freedom and autonomy most characteristic of modern religion are highly valued.[2]

The distinction made in the first chapter between expressive and descriptive adequacy may serve to provide criteria for direct evaluation of comparative world views as philosophical systems that do not entail the judgment that particular aspects of experience or particular stages of development are always preferable to others. For instance, one can claim, as has been argued above, that a monistic metaphysics, built on a model that is extrapolated from the gamut of human experiences most characteristic of traditional mystics, is inadequate to accurately describe the social nature of the self and the world to which it corresponds. Similarly, the choice of isolated individual agency as definitive of the self and of its counterparts makes it impossible to account for the fabric of human society without recourse to the artifice of the social contract or some similar analogy. Thus it can be argued that the social model of the self is superior for descriptive purposes, and that it is able to comprehend and describe both the individualism and the participation celebrated by the other types.

The argument for the greater descriptive adequacy of the social type does not imply that aspects of human experience, of religious ritual, or of personal discipline that grant prominence to the building of community and to the enjoyment of cooperative plans and fellowship are any more valuable than the experiences of the mystics or the sense of individual isolation and personal responsibility underscored by the existentialists. Each is a valid and important aspect of human experience. One or more may be emphasized by a particular culture and tradition, while another may be virtually ignored.

Smart's *Reasons and Faiths*, as remarked above, is one of the few recent attempts to engage in comparative philosophy of religion. Smart has attempted to display the logical strands in various forms of religious doctrine, and thus has concerned himself with comparative analysis. It is not surprising to find that the two basic strands outlined by Smart correspond roughly to the first two types of the present analysis. He refers to these as the mystical strand and the theistic strand, with theism defined as the worship of an other that stands over against one. Though my analysis has been confined to materials representing recent Western philosophy of religion and theology, emanating from within the Christian tradition, the types that I have isolated correspond to the strands discovered by Smart in his attempt to include Oriental, and especially Indian, traditions in the data from which he draws. Such a parallel suggests that there are particular aspects of human experience that are universal, though they may vary in emphasis from one culture to another and from one person to another within a specific culture, which are expressed in the strands and the types that have been displayed.

Smart rightly argues that the philosophy of religion ought to be neutral with regard to religious doctrine, and not serve an apologetic function for a particular tradition. After this neutrality has been achieved, however, and philosophy of religion has been differentiated from Christian,

Jewish, or Buddhist philosophy, it may be proper, within the philosophy of religion, to evaluate the various strands as one might evaluate other philosophical proposals. Smart understands religious doctrines, and metaphysical schemes generally, to be expressive only, thus rendering any descriptive evaluation inappropriate. I have argued that such doctrines and schemes also claim a descriptive adequacy, and thus can be evaluated according to their suitability for describing our experience.

INTERPRETATION AND RELIGION

After the social type has been shown to be the most adequate for a description of human experience, it must be modified and developed in ways more sophisticated than the analysis provided by Royce. In particular, the notion of interpretation that is central to the third type can be illumined by recent work in philosophy and the social sciences. In the sixty years that have elapsed since the publication of *The Problem of Christianity*, much attention has been devoted to the numerous functions of language, and to the interpretive or cognitive dimension of all experience.

Several recent characterizations of religion have focused on the function of religious symbols, insitutions, and practices in aiding persons to "make sense of" their experience.[3] Although rooted in the epistemological analysis of Kant and in the studies of Max Weber, current interest in the cognitive functions of religion stands in contrast to the dominant approaches of theologians, philosophers, and social scientists during the first half of this century. The recognition of the extent to which persons are motivated by seemingly noncognitive needs and forces, the dominance of positivism and behaviorism in much Anglo-American philosophy and psychology, and the appeal to a noncognitive understanding of revelation and faith in neo-orthodox Protestant theology all contributed to an atmosphere in which the cognitive components of religious symbols and practices were largely ignored. The revival of interest in the cognitive is a valuable corrective.

Clifford Geertz has argued that religious symbols function to correlate a world view and an ethos, an image of the world's construction and a program for human conduct. The heart of the religious way of looking at the world, according to Geertz, "is the conviction that the values one holds are grounded in the inherent structure of reality, that between the way one ought to live and the way things really are there is an unbreakable inner connection."[4] Religious symbols, actions, and institutions serve to maintain a connection between factual beliefs and prescriptions for action. In a similar vein, philosopher D. M. Armstrong has provided an analysis of the nature of belief that takes its bearing from F. P. Ramsey's comment that belief is "a map of neighboring space by which we steer."[5] For both Geertz and Armstrong, beliefs are maps that serve to guide action.

Many scholars would agree that religion functions to resolve anxieties over problems of interpretability that arise at boundary situations in human life and experience.[6] But little attention has been given to the issues involved in rendering such formulations more precise. How do crises of interpretability arise? What kinds of interpretation serve to resolve the anxieties associated with these crises? Is the reference to resolution of anxiety an attempt to reduce an essentially cognitive problem to noncognitive components? What is the relation between the cognitive aspects of the need to make sense of one's own experience, and the conative or affective aspects? How important are cognitive factors in enabling one to face a particular crisis? Such issues have been addressed by anthropologists who have focused on crises of interpretability in particular cultures, and similar questions are being raised by social psychologists, but these inquiries have not been brought directly to bear on the study of religion.

The increased interest in the cognitive dimension of religious language underscores the importance of what I have called the descriptive function of the conceptions of God and the self examined in this study. It is becoming increasingly difficult to treat such conceptions as solely expressive. To view them merely as symptoms of particular aspects or stages of experience would be to ignore their cognitive functions. John Bowker has noted the irony of the renewed interest in cognitive issues on the part of social scientists at a time when many students of religion, influenced by earlier approaches in psychology and sociology, have abandoned philosophical and theological analyses in favor of noncognitive approaches.[7] It may be the case that interest in the interpretive function of religious symbols, and in traditional theological and philosophical concerns, will be more evident among social scientists than among theologians.

The processes by which religious symbols function as interpretations of experience, enabling a person to make sense of his world, must be explored on the psychological, social, and cultural levels. Classical and contemporary work in the sociology of knowledge and in cultural anthropology has contributed substantially to our knowledge of the ways in which symbols function. The contribution of structuralism in anthropology, especially the work of Lévi-Strauss and Douglas, has been particularly stimulating for the study of religion. Until recently, however, little attention has been given to the process of interpretation at the level of the individual. The dominant theoretical forces in twentieth-century psychology, behaviorism and psychoanalysis, were both ill-suited to attend to such questions. Behaviorism, as a matter of principle, did not consider beliefs or experiences of any kind, whether religious or secular. Psychoanalysis, following Freud's early lead, tended to treat religion as a collective neurosis and an expression of childish dependency. Although Jung and others in the psychoanalytic tradition have been interested in religious symbolism, most of their work has been clinical in orientation and has neither influenced nor been influenced by the major trends in academic psychology.

In the course of this study I have noted that the ontogenetic analysis offered by psychoanalytic theorists can be helpful in enabling one to discern particular aspects of experience that are expressed by each of the conceptions. While this is appropriate for attention to the expressive function of the conceptions, it is unable to illumine the cognitive or interpretive function.

If religious symbols serve to provide interpretations or at least to resolve crises of interpretability at the boundary situations of human experience (e.g., birth, death, the limits of our understanding, and the limits of our suffering), it is important to consider the strategies open to the individual on such occasions. One response to the anxieties attendant on crises of interpretability has been an appeal to the immediacy of experience. We have seen how both the monistic and the individualistic conceptions include an ideal portrayal of perfect knowledge and action as immediate, unscathed by the institutions of language and society. Such conceptions exert an attraction, particularly in periods in which the cognitive structures or interpretations that have informed a tradition no longer seem compelling. As traditional authorities lose their power to convict, some persons seek refuge in the self-authenticating character of religious experience. By appeal to such experience, the responsibility of interpretation and construction appears to be lifted, and the quest for certainty, for a touchstone that can be trusted, is satisfied. Recent interest among American adolescents in various exotic religious traditions has centered on those traditions which offer relatively clearly defined experiences in which an immediate contact with ultimate reality can be achieved.

An important new resource for understanding the process of interpretation at the individual level is afforded by attribution theory, a new constellation of theoretical approaches in social psychology.[8] The roots of attribution theory can be traced back to William James, in whose work philosophical and psychological issues were closely related. Attribution theory is designed to describe the ways in which persons perceive the causes of their own behavior and of events that befall them. It is directed to the exploration of the labels or attributions employed by individuals in making sense of their experience. This approach is particularly attractive to the student of religion because it is concerned with beliefs, with conceptions of the self, and with the ways in which a person interprets his world.

A central component in the loose coalition known as attribution theory is the work of Stanley Schachter on the emotions. Schachter takes his cue from a theory of the emotions set forth by James in his *Principles of Psychology*.[9] According to Schachter's interpretation and revision of the James-Lange theory, emotional experience includes two components: (1) physiological arousal, and (2) cognitive labeling or interpretation. In a series of related experiments, Schachter and others have shown that emotions such as joy, anger, love, and fear, which have been taken by some to be irreducible, can be broken down into common physiological components and differentiating interpretations.[10] By manipulating the cognitive context of a common arousal, Schachter has shown that emotions, or rather the labels that persons employ to interpret their experiences, can be affected in predictable ways.

The significance of this work for the concerns of the present study is as a demonstration of the role of interpretation at fundamental levels of experience, levels often held to be irreducible. This research can aid us in understanding the conditions under which persons attribute particular labels to themselves and to others. By manipulating the cognitive context, it is possible to affect a subject's understanding of what it is that is being done to him, and thus to introduce a differentiating element into his interpretation of his experience.

This theory of emotion, and further work underway in attribution theory and in self-perception theory, are consistent with the views of Peirce, Royce, Mead, and others who have characterized the development of the self as a process of interpretation of one's own behavior and of the responses of others.[11] An implication of this work is that much of the attention directed to the "essential quality" of particular emotions and experiences by phenomenologists of religion may be misguided. The attempt to delineate the essence of the holy or the sacred, in the manner of Otto, Eliade, and other phenomenologists, may reflect a reification of particular interpretive structures. Mary Douglas has made a similar point by juxtaposing a piece by Husserl on "the essence of redness" with an examination of color perception in Africa, which demonstrates the parochial character of what Husserl took to be a bare, unadorned perception.[12] Increased attention to interpretation will involve relinquishing the goal of immediate experience valued so highly by the phenomenologists.

PHILOSOPHY AND THEOLOGY

In recent theoretical writing, the distinction between expressive and descriptive adequacy has been ignored. Visions, dramatic images, and slogans, appropriate as expressions of particular aspects of personal and cultural experience, have been reified and made to do the work of fundamental philosophical categories. The "death of God" is followed by theologies of hope, of play, and of story. Recent claims for the appropriateness of narrative or story as a fundamental mode of theological discourse draw on the temporal and communal aspects of the social type, while neglecting the issues involved in articulating the metaphysical implications of such a position.[13] The interest in story appears to be an advance from the language of confessionalism and individual self-understanding to a recognition of social communication. Temporal and social contexts are affirmed, but the notion of story remains at the level of expression of particular aspects of experience, and does not move on to the formulation of a new language of description. Such a move would demand consideration of the sociology of knowledge and of the transmission of stories, joining again the issues addressed by Royce's doctrine of interpretation.

While recent claims for the appropriateness of narrative or story as the primary mode of theology include the temporal and discursive elements of the social type and attend to the interpretive role of religious symbols, the manner in which they are employed often conflates the language of expression and the language of description. Or the claim is made that theology is merely expression and is not concerned with descriptive tasks. The present interest in story has arisen as a contemporary version of the claim that religious and theological language is confessional language, and is rooted in H. R. Niebuhr's *The Meaning of Revelation*, but it can also be traced to Barth's use of the term *saga* to signify a genre lying somewhere between myth and history.[14] As confessional language, story does not entail cognitive claims that can be put forth in the public forum. It is the expression of the experience of a person or community. The expressive function of narrative is incontestable, but in order to provide an appropriate analysis of the function of theological language, it would be necessary to move beyond the expressive character to a new language of description. This would involve secondary reflection on the primary language of story. Such a move is resisted, however, by those who would relegate the descriptive task to philosophy and preserve the expressive character of theology.

One of the indications of the roots in the confessional tradition of the proposal that theological language be understood primarily as narrative is the attempt to sharply distinguish such narrative from the analytical language of philosophical inquiry. The implication is that strict limits can be set to questions that can appropriately be asked about theological conceptions. These conceptions are held to function in an arena unscathed by secondary or analytical considerations.

While the paradigmatic statement of the separation of philosophy from theology in the modern period has been made by Karl Barth, this position has been recently defended by Stephen Crites in an article that is significant both because it makes explicit a common presupposition in much contemporary theology and philosophy of religion, and because Crites is one of the most careful and perceptive of those who are claiming that the proper form of theological expression is narrative.[15]

Crites makes four major points: (1) philosophy and theology, when properly practiced, employ different modes of certification; (2) philosophical truths are certified by implicit appeal to an ideal community of rational observers, and theological truths by appeal to specific historical communities; (3) participation and commitment are demanded of the theologian, while the philosopher must attain and maintain aesthetic distance; and (4) theology reflects the primary structure of religious language, which is narrative.

The first point is crucial. Different processes of certification, and thus different criteria of truth, are appropriate in philosophy and theology. Theological and philosophical statements appeal to different notions of truth, and thus can never conflict. This claim is associated with Averroes and has been defended in different forms by Spinoza and Schleiermacher.[16] To accept such a sharp distinction, however, is to ignore the continuous process of interpretation and integration that we have seen to be a characteristic of the social conception.

We listen, speak, and think in one language. We may master a second language, but the language that we speak is all of a piece. Our words receive their meanings as part of a linguistic field or fabric. The public meanings that we learn and to which we are faithful, the novelty created by the imaginative juxtapositions of the poet, and the neologisms of technology are all parts of this fabric.

Wittgenstein once compared language to a city:

Our language can be seen as an ancient city: a maze of little streets and squares, of old and new houses, and of houses with

additions from various periods; and this surrounded by a mul-
titude of new boroughs with straight regular streets and uni-
form houses.[17]

Such a city might include streets, alleys, highways, and even
some walls, but there would be no complete discontinuity.
The position articulated by Crites regarding the relation of
philosophy and theology would demand that a wall be
erected in the city of our language, such that no commerce
would be permitted across this wall.

Such formulations propose a fundamental equivocity in
the use of language, a wall on either side of which words are
employed in different senses. Often the placing of this wall
is based on a distinction between existential participant and
detached observer. Such a distinction is reified until it becomes a separation and can be appealed to in support of a
claim for discontinuity between two sectors of the language.
Thus it is assured that statements in one sector will remain
unscathed by critical questions framed in another sector.

This equivocity raises problems concerning the personal
and social identities of language users. The city of one's
language is also the *polis* in which he or she constructs an
identity as a kind of political unity. This unity is constructed, in part, by the use of stories and narratives of
personal history. In part it is created by viewing oneself
from the point of view of another, and by reviewing events
in retrospect with an attitude approaching analytical detachment. A sense of "I," as Mead has suggested, is not
alone a first-person experience, but is affected and corrected by a sense of "me," the object of the observations of
oneself and of others.[18] Both nominative and accusative
constructions are part of the same language. They lie in the
city that a person attempts to order or map in the construction of an identity.

Granted that religious belief often arises within experiences that are highly personal, such as the mystic's sense of
union with the whole, or an experience of alienation from

or encounter with another, it is still necessary to integrate such personal experience into one's mapping of himself in relation to his world. The experience must be interpreted. Some interpretation, of course, has already taken place. But it is necessary to carry the process further in order to integrate powerful personal experiences with the demands and opportunities of mundane reality. A task of the philosopher or the theologian is to aid in this process, to demonstrate conflicts between the implications of several parochial concerns, and to propose a more inclusive scheme in which each of the experiences has its integrity within a coherent context.

When an individual awakens to a new sense of himself or herself, he or she must integrate this new sense with other experiences and self-concepts. Integration may not be easy, but it is impossible to maintain separate sectors of language, mind, or experience. We all try. We repress experiences and deny self-knowledge, but these are all maneuvers in the processes of integration. If one's entire life and language were ensconced within an actual historical community so that the community was congruent in one's mind with the regulative idea of an assembly of rational observers, no difficulty would arise. But we all live and participate in a variety of communities, roles, and identities. It is a feature of the secularization of the modern world that processes of integration have become more self-conscious than they were in earlier periods.

The distinction Crites has drawn between philosophy and theology is a reification of Kant's distinction between the theoretical and the practical. The distinction drawn in the present work between descriptive and expressive adequacy may seem to be a similar one, but there are some crucial differences. Both the expressive and descriptive tasks are practical ones involving the construction of particular interpretations. The distinction is drawn between different functions, both of which may be served by the same language. It is not drawn between different language games or strata. The functions cannot be sharply separated, though they can be distinguished. The force of a particular conception as the expression of the experience of a person or culture is bound to affect the choice of a basic descriptive model. Different criteria can be specified, but the functions can never be completely separated. Theological doctrines must be subject to the criteria for descriptive adequacy if they are to be integrated with our other constructions or maps of our world.

The defense of the nonphilosophical character of theology is designed to purchase the autonomy of theology, but this purchase may be made at the expense of its relation to other aspects of our experience. The present distinction between expressive and descriptive adequacy recognizes a difference in function without denying the public community of interpretation. While religious language may involve narrative and witness as well as confession, praise, and exhortation, theology as secondary language is more akin to philosophy. It is an attempt to reflect upon, describe, and criticize the language of religion as philosophy reflects upon. describes, and criticizes linguistic usage in other areas of our common speech.

THE SELF AND GOD AS INTERPRETATIONS

What, then, is the philosophy of religion? It is the rational reconstruction of concepts that originate in the symbols and practices that constitute religious experience. These symbols and practices are those which enable a person or a culture to deal with crises of interpretability as these arise in limiting or boundary situations. Examples of the limits at which such crises of interpretability arise are: (1) the limits of his analytic capacities, (2) the limits of his powers of endurance, and (3) the limits of his moral insight.[19] Such crises arise in response to birth, death, experiences of awe or wonder, periods of cultural transition and the waning of traditional authorities, and in other situations in which a person is aware of the limits of his interpretive powers.

Theology is the same kind of rational reconstruction, but it is one in which the conception of God is central. Theology is not defined in terms of a particular community and its doctrine. This latter notion of theology, reflected in Crites's separation of theology and philosophy, has been current in much of Protestant thought since Schleiermacher, but it results in an abdication of responsibility for public debate concerning the descriptive adequacy of theological conceptions. The effect is to assimilate theology to the language of confession, and thus to one among the several forms of primary religious language (e.g., prayer, sermon, hymn, memoir) in a particular religious community. The language of religion contains much primary language of this sort, but theology aspires to a more public and comprehensive reconstruction.

This understanding of the task of philosophy of religion and theology is not new, though it certainly does not represent an explicit consensus of those working in the field. The point to be emphasized here, however, is the nature of philosophy of religion and theology as rational construction or reconstruction. They represent forms of interpretation of the sort that has here been considered under the rubric of the social type. In a post-Kantian context, theology cannot be seen as a direct description of some external world with which we can make direct contact. It is rather an attempt to construct interpretations of God, the self, the world, and appropriate categories for describing our experiences in that world. Our very ability to construct interpretations and to take responsibility for them must also be accounted for in our understanding of ourselves and our worlds.

One of the chief characteristics of modern religion and theology is the fact that theologians and religious folk have become increasingly aware of their own responsibility for their religious symbols and practices. Such symbols and practices are recognized as social constructions or interpretations. Many have tried to foresee what this increased self-consciousness might mean for the life of religious symbols. Some have claimed that man has "come of age" and is engaged in a gradual process of secularization that will end with release from religious world views. Religion is seen as a sign of man's immaturity.[20] Others have argued that only the forms have changed, but that religious orientation of some kind is fundamental to human experience. Robert Bellah, a proponent of this latter view, has devoted considerable attention to the ways in which religious symbols can continue to provide orientation and a basis for trust even when understood as social constructions.

Theology, then, along with metaphysics generally, is to be seen as construction. Conceptions of the self and God are interpretations that we construct in order to aid us in making sense of our experience. But how self-conscious are we about this process of construction? It is here that the earlier distinction between expressive and descriptive functions becomes relevant once again. The monistic type and the individualistic type, as expressions of the experience of mystical union and of a claim standing over against one, are constructions, as is the social type. Insofar as they are primarily expressive of certain aspects of experience that are particularly salient, however, they are constructions that are relatively spontaneous. They arise from the experience itself and they commend themselves to us by capturing a vision, or by striking us as particularly fitting. They are *relatively* spontaneous. No expression is utterly spontaneous, and sophisticated works of art are often expressions that are the products of the most rigorous discipline and painstaking care. But the criteria by which we judge a work of art or even a set of religious symbols as expressions of certain aspects of experience are related to the degree to which they seem to capture that experience. Such works commend themselves to an audience by the richness with which they convey the felt immediacy and the interpretive depths of such experience.

While most, if not all, metaphysical or theological constructs have their origin in such "fitting" expressions, the adequacy of a particular conception for describing an experience in ways that can be integrated with our other cognitions and interpretations of the world must be judged in a more self-conscious and reflective mood. For this latter task, the immediate sense of the fitting provides insight, but not the final criteria. Comprehensiveness, the ability to interpret all aspects of our own experience and that of others without declaring some experiences invalid because they do not fit into the vision, and coherence are necessary. The concepts and theories resulting from such reflection are social constructs fully as much as are those which express particular aspects of experience. They are constructions that are continually being revised in the light of new experience.

Conceptions of God and the self are constructions that attempt to describe the limits of our experience. Kant described them as regulative ideas. The self stands at the limit that is the origin of our acts, and is thus inaccessible to us in our thinking or action. A conception of God stands at the limit of our ability to imagine the origin and goal of all experience. These constructions are necessarily constantly receding, and must always be redefined so as to stand at the limits of experience. When either becomes reified or reduced to something within experience, it no longer can serve as a regulative idea and thus no longer functions as a symbol of God or the self.

Because conceptions of God and the self function as limiting constructs, the distinction between their functions as expressive and descriptive is difficult to keep in focus. If such constructs do not commend themselves to us as fitting, they cannot serve their religious functions. Tillich has vividly described the birth and death of religious symbols. Geertz has focused on the points at which men are no longer grasped by particular symbols, but grasp at them in a futile effort to keep them from losing their authority. Yet that which grasps a person or community must eventually be subjected to the criteria that are applied to other cognitive constructions and must be integrated into our understanding of ourselves and of our experience. Religious or theological symbols may be experienced as self-authenticating in their immediacy. But in order to function as proper theological constructions they must also be subject to the criteria appropriate to descriptive theories.

When the monistic and the individualistic types are subjected to the criterion of comprehensiveness, they are found wanting in their ability to provide an adequate account of the experience of social reality, and particularly of time and language. The social model, while rooted in a particular expression, is sufficiently comprehensive to take account of the experiences that give rise to the other two types, and to account as well for the social character of our experience.

The social conception of the self and the correlative conception of God are the most promising for a theological or metaphysical analysis that can serve the purposes of description as well as expression. An implication of this third type and of the present emphasis upon theology as construction is that the self and God are themselves constructions. Royce writes that the self is not a datum, but an interpretation. He is ambiguous about the issue as to whether God is to be conceived as the interpreter or interpretation of the beloved community. To be consistent with the implications of the third type, both the self and God must be understood as interpretive constructions.

One of the frustrations attendant upon a perusal of recent psychological literature on the self results from the fact that most research has been concerned with self-concepts rather than with the nature of the self. If we follow the lead of William James, however, and the implications of the notion of interpretation proposed by Peirce and Royce, it may be that the self is an interpretation, and thus there is no real distinction between self and self-concept. Self-concepts that are the objects of psychological research may have been too narrowly defined, but the self is an interpretation or a reflexive concept. The ability of an organism to symbolize its own behavior and that of others is developed in the course of the growth of an individual as it has developed phylogenetically. One cannot speak of a self being present before the organism learns to interpret its own behavior and to reflect on itself. Mead has given considerable attention to the processes by which this symbolic behavior and self-reflection develop. The concept of the self, and thus the self, emerge as a construct based on the perception of one's own actions, directly and through the eyes of others.

When both God and the self are understood to be interpretations, one can readily see how the various conceptions that have been examined in this study might arise in different contexts. It then becomes clear that criteria are needed to enable persons to choose the most adequate construction for descriptive purposes, just as such criteria are needed for the choice between competing constructions in other aspects of our experience.

NOTES

1. See Ninian Smart, *Reasons and Faiths* (London: Routledge and Kegan Paul), p. 4.

2. Robert Bellah, "Religious Evolution," *Beyond Belief* (New York: Harper and Row, 1970), pp. 20–50.

3. For example, Mary Douglas, *Purity and Danger* (London: Routledge and Kegan Paul, 1966); Bellah, *Beyond Belief*; and Clifford Geertz, *The Interpretation of Cultures* (New York: Basic Books, 1973).

4. Clifford Geertz, *Islam Observed* (New Haven, Conn.: Yale University Press, 1968), p. 97.

5. D. M. Armstrong, *Belief, Truth and Knowledge* (London: Cambridge University Press, 1973), p. 3.

6. See, for example, David Little and Sumner Twiss, Jr., "Basic Terms in the Study of Religious Ethics," in Gene Outka and John Reeder, Jr., eds., *Religion and Morality* (Garden City, N. Y.: Doubleday, 1973), pp. 35–77.

7. John Bowker, *The Sense of God* (Oxford: The Clarendon Press, 1973).

8. Wayne Proudfoot and Phillip Shaver, "Attribution Theory and the Psychology of Religion," *Journal for The Scientific Study of Religion* 14 (1975): 317–30.

9. William James, *The Principles of Psychology* (New York: Henry Holt, 1890), 2: 442–85.

10. Stanley Schachter, *Emotion, Obesity and Crime* (New York: Academic Press, 1971).

11. For a discussion of other components of attribution theory and of self-perception theory, see Proudfoot and Shaver, "Attribution Theory and the Psychology of Religion."

12. Mary Douglas, ed., *Rules and Meanings* (London: Penguin, 1973), pp. 60–69.

13. See, for example, John Dunne, *A Search for God in Time and Memory* (New York: The Macmillan Company, 1972). Also Stephen Crites, "The Narrative Quality of Experience," *Journal of the American Academy of Religion* 39 (1971): 291–311. Crites's article is the most careful and sophisticated of the recent literature on story.

14. H. Richard Niebuhr, *The Meaning of Revelation* (New York: The Macmillan Company, 1941); Karl Barth, *Church Dogmatics*, ed., G. W. Bromiley and T. F. Torrance (Edinburgh: T. & T. Clark, 1958), 3/1: 81–94.

15. Stephen Crites, "Five Philosophical Points on the Non-Philosophical Character of Theology: A Neo-Averroist View," *Soundings* 54 (1970): 187–207.

16. Baruch Spinoza, "Theologico-Political Treatise," *Works of Spinoza*, trans. R. W. Elwes (New York: Dover, 1951), 1: 189; Friedrich Schleiermacher, *The Christian Faith*, ed., H. R. Mackintosh and J. S. Stewart (New York: Harper and Row, 1953), 1:83.

17. Ludwig Wittgenstein, *Philosophical Investigations*, trans. G. E. M. Anscombe (New York: Macmillan, 1953), par. 8.

18. George Herbert Mead, *Mind, Self and Society*, ed., C. W. Morris (Chicago: The University of Chicago Press, 1934), pp. 173–78.

19. See, for example, Clifford Geertz, "Religion as a Cultural System," *The Interpretation of Cultures*.

20. Critics of theology and theologians have both proclaimed the end of the religious age. See, for example, Sigmund Freud, *The Future of an Illusion*, ed., J. Strachey (Garden City, N. Y.: Doubleday, 1964); Dietrich Bonhoeffer, *Letters and Papers from Prison*, ed., E. Bethge (New York: The Macmillan Company, 1953).

Bibliography

Adams, James Luther. *Paul Tillich's Philosophy of Culture, Science and Religion*. New York: Harper and Row, 1965.

Allport, Gordon W. *Becoming*. New Haven: Yale University Press, 1954.

Armstrong, D. M. *Belief, Truth and Knowledge*. London: Cambridge University Press, 1973.

Barth, Karl. *Church Dogmatics*. Edited by G. W. Bromiley and T. F. Torrance. 4 vols. Edinburgh: T. & T. Clark, 1936–60.

Bellah, Robert N. *Beyond Belief: Essays on Religion in a Post-Traditional World*. New York: Harper and Row, 1970.

Bonhoeffer, Dietrich. *Letters and Papers from Prison*. Edited by E. Bethge. New York: The Macmillan Company, 1953.

Bowker, John. *The Sense of God*. Oxford: The Clarendon Press, 1973.

Brown, Norman O. *Love's Body*. New York: Random House, 1966.

Buber, Martin. *I and Thou*. Translated by R. G. Smith. Edinburgh: T. & T. Clark, 1937.

Cairns, David. *The Image of God in Man*. London: Student Christian Movement Press, 1953.

Calvin, John. *Institutes of the Christian Religion*. Edited by J. McNeill; translated by F. Battles. Philadelphia: The Westminster Press, 1960.

Coleridge, Samuel Taylor. *Aids to Reflection*. Edited by J. Marsh. Burlington, Vt.: Chauncey Goodrich, 1829.

Cotton, J. Harry. *Royce on the Human Self*. Cambridge, Mass.: Harvard University Press, 1954.

Crites, Stephen D. "Five Philosophical Points on the Non-Philosophical Character of Theology: A Neo-Averroist View." *Soundings* 54 (1970): 187–207.

————. "The Narrative Quality of Experience." *Journal of he American Academy of Religion* 39 (1971): 291–311.

Douglas, Mary. *Purity and Danger*. London: Routledge and Kegan Paul, 1966.

————, ed. *Rules and Meanings*. London: Penguin, 1973.

Dunne, John S. *A Search for God in Time and Memory*. New York: The Macmillan Company, 1967.

————. *The Way of All the Earth*. New York: The Macmillan Company, 1972.

Duval, Shelley, and Wicklund, Robert A. *A Theory of Objective Self-Awareness*. New York: Academic Press, 1972.

Edwards, Jonathan. *The Works of President Edwards: With a Memoir of His Life*. Edited by S. E. Dwight. New York: G. & C. & H. Carvill, 1830.

Eliade, Mircea. *Cosmos and History: The Myth of the Eternal Return*. Translated by W. R. Trask. New York: Harper and Row, 1959.

Emmet, Dorothy. *The Nature of Metaphysical Thinking*. London: Macmillan and Company, 1945.

Erikson, Erik H. *Childhood and Society*. 2d ed. New York: W. W. Norton and Company, 1963.

Farrer, Austin M. *Faith and Speculation*. New York: New York University Press, 1967.

————. *Finite and Infinite*, Second edition. London: Dacre Press, 1959.

————. *The Freedom of the Will*. New York: Charles Scribner's Sons, 1958.

————. *The Glass of Vision*. London: Dacre Press, 1948.

————. *A Rebirth of Images: The Making of St. John's Apocalypse*. London: Dacre Press, 1949.

Flew, Antony, and MacIntyre, Alasdair, eds. *New Essays in Philosophical Theology*. London: Student Christian Movement Press, 1955.

Freud, Sigmund. *The Future of an Illusion*. Translated by J. Strachey. Garden City, New York: Doubleday, 1964.

Geertz, Clifford. *Islam Observed*. New Haven: Yale University Press, 1968.

————. *The Interpretation of Cultures*. New York: Basic Books, 1973.

Glasse, John. "Doing Theology Metaphysically: Austin Farrer." *Harvard Theological Review* 59 (1966): 319–50.

Goffman, Erving. *The Presentation of Self in Everyday Life*. New York: Doubleday, 1959.

Hare, Richard M. *The Language of Morals*. London: Oxford University Press, 1952.

Hartshorne, Charles. *The Divine Relativity: A Social Conception of God*. New Haven: Yale University Press, 1948.

Hegel, Georg Wilhelm Friedrich. *Reason in History*. Translated by R. S. Hartman. New York: Bobbs-Merrill, 1953.

Hook, Sidney, ed. *Religious Experience and Truth: A Symposium*. New York: New York University Press, 1961.

James, William. *Pragmatism*. New York: Longmans, Green and Company, 1907.

———. *The Principles of Psychology*. 2 vols. New York: Henry Holt and Company, 1890.

Kant, Immanuel. *Critique of Pure Reason*. Edited by Norman K. Smith. London: Macmillan and Company, 1933.

———. *Foundations of the Metaphysics of Morals*. Translated by L. W. Beck. New York: The Liberal Arts Press, 1959.

Lévi-Strauss, Claude. *Structural Anthropology*. Translated by C. Jacobson and B. G. Schoepf. Garden City, N. Y.: Doubleday, 1967.

Little, David, and Twiss, Sumner B., Jr. "Basic Terms in the Study of Religious Ethics," in Gene Outka and John Reeder, Jr., eds. *Religion and Morality*. Garden City, N.Y.: Doubleday, 1973.

May, Rollo; Angel, Ernest; and Ellenberger, Henri F., eds. *Existence: A New Dimension in Psychiatry and Psychology*. New York: Basic Books, Company, 1958.

Mead, George Herbert. *Mind, Self, and Society*. Edited by C. Morris. Chicago: University of Chicago Press, 1934.

Neumann, Erich. *The Origins and History of Consciousness*. Translated by R. F. C. Hull. Pantheon, 1954.

Neville, Robert. "Some Historical Problems About the Transcendence of God." *The Journal of Religion* 47 (1967): 1–9.

Niebuhr, H. Richard. *The Meaning of Revelation*. New York: The Macmillan Company, 1941.

Parsons, Talcott. *The Structure of Social Action*. 2 vols. New York: The Free Press, A Division of The Macmillan Company, 1968.

Peirce, Charles Sanders. *Collected Papers of Charles Sanders Peirce*, vols. 5–6. Edited by C. Hartshorne and P. Weiss. Cambridge, Mass. Harvard University Press, 1934–35.

Proudfoot, Wayne, and Shaver, Phillip. "Attribution Theory and the Psychology of Religion." *Journal for the Scientific Study of Religion* 14 (1975): 317–30.

von Rad, Gerhard. *Studies in Deuteronomy*. Translated by D. Stalker. London: Student Christian Movement Press, 1956.

Royce, Josiah. *The Philosophy of Loyalty*. New York: The Macmillan Company, 1908.

———. *The Problem of Christianity*. 2 vols. New York: The Macmillan Company, 1913.

———. *The Religious Aspect of Philosophy*. Boston: Houghton Mifflin Company, 1885.

———. *The Sources of Religious Insight*. New York: Charles Scribner's Sons, 1913.

———. *The World and the Individual*. 2 vols. New York: The Macmillan Company, 1899, 1901.

Sarbin, Theodore R. "A Preface to a Psychological Analysis of the Self." *Psychological Review* 59 (1952): 11–22.

Schachter, Stanley. *Emotion, Obesity and Crime*. New York: Academic Press, 1971.

Schleiermacher, Friedrich Daniel Ernst. *The Christian Faith*. Translated by H. R. Mackintosh and J. S. Stewart. Edinburgh: T. & T. Clark, 1928.

Slater, Philip. *Microcosm: Structural, Psychological and Religious Evolution in Groups*. New York: John Wiley and Sons, 1966.

———. *The Pursuit of Loneliness: American Culture at the Breaking Point*. Boston: Beacon Press, 1970.

———. "Toward a Dualistic Theory of Identification." *Merrill-Palmer Quarterly* 7 (1961): 113–26.

Smart, Ninian. *Reasons and Faiths*. London: Routledge and Kegan Paul, 1958.

Smith, John E. *Royce's Social Infinite*. New York: The Liberal Arts Press, 1950.

Spinoza, Benedict. *Works of Spinoza*. Translated by R. H. M. Elwes. 2 vols. New York: Dover, 1951.

Tillich, Paul. *The Courage to Be*. New Haven, Conn.: Yale University Press, 1952.

———. *Dynamics of Faith*. New York: Harper and Brothers, 1957.

———. "Participation and Knowledge: Problems of an Ontology

of Cognition." *Sociologica*. Aufsätze, Max Horkheimer zum sechzigsten Geburtstag gewidmet. (Vol. I: "Frankfurter Beiträge zur Sociologie," edited by Theodor W. Adorno and Walter Dirks.) Frankfort am Main: Europäische Verlagsanstalt, 1955. pp. 201–209.

————. *The Protestant Era*. Edited by J. L. Adams. Chicago: University of Chicago Press, 1948.

————. *The Shaking of the Foundations*. New York: Charles Scribner's Sons, 1948.

————. *Systematic Theology*. 3 vols. Chicago: University of Chicago Press, 1951–1963.

————. "Die Theologie des Kairos und die gegenwärtige geistige Lage: Offener Brief an Emmanuel Hirsch." Theologische Blätter 13 (1934): 305–28.

Tillich, Paul. *The Theology of Culture*. Edited by R. C. Kimball. New York: Oxford University Press, 1959.

Weber, Max. *The Methodology of the Social Sciences*. Translated by E. Shils and H. Finch. New York: The Free Press of Glencoe, 1949.

Wittgenstein, Ludwig. *Philosophical Investigations*. Translated by G. E. M. Anscombe. New York: The Macmillan Company, 1953.

————. *Tractatus Logico-Philosophicus*. Translated by C. K. Ogden and F. P. Ramsey. London: Routledge and Kegan Paul, Ltd., 1922.

Wolff, Peter H. "The Developmental Psychologies of Jean Piaget and Psychoanalysis." *Psychological Issues*, 2, no. 1. New York: International Universities Press, 1960.

Wright, George Ernest. *God Who Acts*. London: Student Christian Movement Press, 1952.

Index

239